Love
Italian
Style

Love Italian Style

The Secrets of My Hot and Happy Marriage

MELISSA GORGA

ST. MARTIN'S PRESS ❧ NEW YORK

Photographs: pages 118, 173 by Jason Russo/HeyMrJason Photography; page 200 by
Michael Simon; page 234 by Manny Carabell/MTC Photography. All other photos
courtesy of the author.

www.stmartins.com

Design by Steven Seighman

Library of Congress Cataloging-in-Publication Data

Gorga, Melissa.
    Love Italian style : the secrets of my hot and happy marriage / Melissa Gorga.—First
edition.
        pages cm
    ISBN 978-1-250-04148-7 (hardcover)
    ISBN 978-1-4668-3798-0 (e-book)
  1. Gorga, Melissa.   2. Married people.   3. Man-woman relationships.   4. Marital
quality.   I. Title.
    HQ734.G665 2013
    306.872—dc23

                                                                            2013020559

St. Martin's Press books may be purchased for educational, business, or promotional
use. For information on bulk purchases, please contact Macmillan Corporate and Pre-
mium Sales Department at 1-800-221-7945, extension 5442, or write specialmarkets
@macmillan.com.

First Edition: September 2013

10 9 8 7 6 5 4 3 2 1

Dedicated to the two men in my life—

My father: I wish you could have walked me down the aisle and met my three little angels. Now you're my angel, watching over all of us. I love you, Daddy. If only you could have met Joe.

My handsome husband and the love of my life: You have put me on a pedestal since day one. You have kept all of your promises. You are more than any woman could ever ask for. I love you more and more each day.

Contents

• CONTENTS •

Love
Italian
Style

INTRODUCTION

· ·

Blueprint for a Better Marriage

ince I entered the world of reality TV, the number one message I get from fans is, "I want your marriage!" Strange women come up to Joe on the street and say, "I wish my husband still grabbed at *me*!" At events, fans confide to me, "I love how you look at each other." It can feel a little embarrassing that our private life is exposed. But I'm genuinely thrilled that our laughter and passion has made as big an impression as the nasty catfights on display, every day, on *The Real Housewives of New Jersey*.

The number two message I get from fans: "How do you *do* it?"

I firmly believe that any woman can have as much passion, fun, and commitment as I have with Joe, as long as she's willing to make the effort. A great marriage doesn't just happen. It's a job. I work on my marriage every single day. God knows, our relationship hasn't always been perfect. Nothing is perfect. However, what makes it come close is personal motivation. I *want* a happy, respectful, and passionate marriage. That desire drives me to be a better wife and friend to Joe. If other women *want* a close-to-perfect marriage, they can have it, too. It's their choice. Even if they don't think they are, *they are in control.* Women steer the ship. What they say and how they act towards their partner will directly correlate with his response. I also want women to know that it is a process. A bad marriage today can be a great one tomorrow. It took me a good five years to really figure out Joe, the nuances of our relationship, what triggers our happiness, anger, frustration, and that our everyday fights are rooted in nonsense. Every year, the learning curve has flattened. And now that Joe and I are running smoother than ever, I want to share my winning playbook with all women.

On these pages, I explain everything I've learned and everything I do to make my marriage work. I make my husband the happiest man on the planet, which, in turn, makes me feel like the luckiest woman alive. Readers can take what they want from my experience, and leave what they don't. I'm not telling anyone how to live. I can only describe how I do things, and what I believe makes our marriage as sexy and hot as it is warm and loving.

For starters, my number one, overriding "Gorganizing" principle of how to have a passionate and happy marriage is to treat your husband like a King.

What the . . . ? Treat your husband like a King? Are we in the Dark Ages?

I get that. Whenever I say the King line to a new person, I brace myself for the "She's crazy!" or "How sad for her" looks. For the first few years of our marriage, I got caught up in the concept of being an old-fashioned wife, too.

He wanted me to cook and clean? Of course, I want my family to eat well. Nothing makes me feel more satisfied. Of course, I like a nice house. But it felt different and somehow wrong when Joe told me I had to.

He wanted me to run to the door when he got home? Yes, I was excited to see my husband at the end of the day. But rushing to greet him when he came in felt like I was at his beck and call.

Sex on demand? Not a chance. I was all for having a lot of sex, but it had to be when we both wanted it.

Was I his wife, or his slave?

We would get locked in power struggles about this stuff. I'd been raised to be a strong, independent woman, and I was definitely not going to cater to his every whim. In the first couple of years, my pride always seemed to get in the way.

I had to break down my defensive wall, and understand that it was a matter of perception. When we started dating, all I cared about was making Joe happy. After we got married, Joe told me exactly what would make him happy, and I sometimes would misinterpret his directness as demands. Make no mistake, Joe also wanted to know what would make me happy, as well. But, for whatever reason, when a man tells a woman what he wants, it can feel like control. The truth is, a relationship is not about control. A relationship *should* be about wanting the best for your partner, bringing out the best in each other, and giving him the best that you have. As soon as I changed my perception about Joe's wants and needs, things immediately improved.

In a flash of insight, I realized that our happiness was my choice. No matter who brought home the pancetta and who fried it up in a pan, we were equal partners. We shared equal responsibility for each other's security and happiness, as well as our own. If I treated him like a King, he'd respond by treating me like a Queen. It was a leap of faith. I'm so glad I made it. I feel blessed by the love, passion, and respect he gives me every day. Tearing down that wall did not require me to swallow my pride or make any sacrifices. There is no such thing as pride in a marriage, except for feeling proud to be together, and of how happy you can make each other.

Wifey? Slave? Subservient? I don't think so. I'm not some throwback desperate housewife who sits around all day in a ratty moomoo waiting for her husband to come home and validate her existence. On RHONJ, do you see me looking like a wreck, hair a mess, moaning and bitching? No. Hey, I wax my mustache. I rock a five-inch Jimmy Choo. In the game of chess, the King can only move one square at a time. The Queen can zip across the board every turn. As the Queen, I create the playbook for our marriage. On our chessboard, I'm zooming up the iTunes charts and performing on concert stages, but I'm never more than one step away from being at my husband's side. What I want women to know is that by embracing some of the old-fashioned values of putting your man on a pedestal, you will actually be the one standing higher up—because you'll end up getting more of what you want.

I know it sounds contradictory. But I'm not a contradiction. *I'm a combination.* I have self-respect, *and* my husband is happy. I'm the class mom, *and* I have a singing career. I'm a housewife, *and* I'm on *Housewives.* I'm rooted in old-school Italian values, while still being a thoroughly modern woman. The food equivalent—it's always about food for Italians—would be using state-of-the-art kitchen gadgets to make a traditional recipe from your great-great-great-great grandmother.

Now, I hear a lot of complaints from wives who feel unappreciated and ignored. The husband doesn't talk to her or look at her, not even when she's dressed up. He comes home, grunts two words and then closes himself in the TV room. He never touches her and turns his back to her in bed. He looks for every excuse to get out with his friends. That does not happen in my house. Why? One word: *King.* Some of my own friends look at how I treat Joe, shake their heads and say, "I'd never do that for my husband. Treat him like a King? Cook him dinner to make *him* feel appreciated? Unless he does for me first, he can go scratch."

A marriage isn't about scorekeeping or payback. When I used to ask, "What have you done for me lately?" I always felt shortchanged. Selfishness in marriage breeds on itself. You focus on what's missing. When I flipped it around to ask, "What can I do for you?" Joe scrambled to reciprocate, and I felt cherished and appreciated. Is there any greater happiness on Earth than making the people you love happy, seeing them smile, and helping them succeed? Not as far as I'm concerned. I don't lose myself by loving and respecting my husband. I get it back times a thousand.

After five years of marriage, Joe and I were still living in our newlywed house in Franklin Lakes. I was always acutely aware that I was a very lucky girl to live there. It was gorgeous. Joe built the 10,000-square-foot house when he was barely twenty-three years old. The only problem: It was on a main road, and we were far from family. I had wanted to move, but we were caught up in our lives and didn't do anything about it.

That Christmas Eve, Joe reached under the tree and dragged out a huge box. "For you," he said. It was surprisingly heavy. Excited and curious, I opened it up, peeled away the inside paper, and found a rock sitting on the bottom of the box.

Not a gold brick.

Not a "rock," as in, a diamond.

It was a dirty, gray paver.

"Oh, thank you?" I said.

Joe laughed. "What's wrapped around it?"

He smoothed out the inside paper on the table. Taking a closer look, I realized it was a set of blueprints.

"This is our new house," he said, grinning, eyes beaming.

"What?" I didn't get it at first, but then he explained. For the last six weeks, Joe had been staying late after work with his friend Ralph, an architect, putting the blueprints together.

In my paranoid moments during those weeks, I worried that Joe didn't want to come home to me. I'd been calling him, asking, "Where are you? With Ralph *again*?" I didn't like Ralph. He went to parties without his wife and lived in strip clubs. Joe had been hanging out with him every night for over a month? Not good. Well, I'd been way off. He hadn't been crooked with Ralph. He'd been designing our dream house, where we'd eat, drink, fight, make love, raise kids, and be together. Is this the best husband, or what? I swore in my heart, that if Joe was going to build me a house, that I was going to build him a home.

Joe built our castle in less than a year, from the shiny parquet floors to the top of the vaulted ceilings, and I decorated every room from the color on each and every wall to the color of the metal on all seven toilet bowl flushers. There is not one inch of this house that is not a piece of us. All that said, as far as I'm concerned, Joe and I could live in a shoe box, and we'd still treat each other like royalty. But, what has taken up most of my time and continues to be my number one priority: building our home, and the way we live and love inside these walls. Like the physical structure, blueprints were needed to design our marriage, too. Ours has a strong foundation and four immovable cornerstones:

RESPECT

If you did a word cloud chart of *Sopranos* dialogue, *respect* would probably get the biggest bubble (well, the second biggest). This one word is overused in the Italian culture because it encompasses so many others, like acknowledgment, gratitude, acceptance, and understanding.

Joe works his ass off. He might be the boss of his construction company, but he gets his hands dirty, tearing out walls or pulling up floors. When he comes home, he wants to be greeted at the door by his wife and kids. He expects a hot meal and a clean house. To him, that's how a wife shows her husband *respect*. It's how he was raised.

When he originally asked for these things, I used to think, *I should reward you for going out and earning a living? That's what you should do! I had a hard day, too.* Joe wasn't asking for a reward, though. He wasn't implying I didn't work hard. He was asking for respect, a simple acknowledgment that he'd been away and had returned. Once I let go of the defensiveness and scorekeeping, I opened my heart to giving him what he needed to feel respected by me. The list is surprisingly short.

WHAT JOE NEEDS TO FEEL RESPECTED BY ME

1. To be greeted at the door with a hug, kiss, and a smile.
2. A home-cooked dinner in a well-kept house with fresh and clean kids.
3. Sex three to five times a week.

Not so hard to do. In return, Joe shows his respect for me by appreciating what I do, praising my efforts, complimenting me, hugging and kissing me, making love to me nearly every night, providing us with a gorgeous house, playing on the floor with the kids, listening to me, looking at me, having my back no matter what, and giving me a deep sense of security. Honestly, I could get by with a lot less.

WHAT I NEED TO FEEL RESPECTED BY JOE

1. He tells me where he is, what he's doing, and with whom.
2. Kind words.
3. Sexy looks.

Considering the huge emotional demands people put on their relationships, what Joe and I require from each other is hardly anything at all, yet it's the world to us. We can count on each other for the basics and so much more.

LOYALTY

Another heavy rotation word among our people. In the context of a marriage, loyalty usually means fidelity. It goes without saying that cheating is not tolerated in my marriage. Fidelity, though, is just the tip of the loyalty iceberg for us. Fans of RHONJ know all too well that Joe will go to war for me. He'll march into battle and slay my enemies. I can call him any time of day or night. He'll drop whatever he's doing, get on his white horse (or a black Range Rover), and race flat-out to my side. No questions, no hesitation. He can't wait to do it! I'd even say he lives for the opportunity. And, I would do the same for him. That's loyalty.

It's about putting family first. Joe and I are each other's sun and moon. Our marriage is what gets us up each morning, and let's us sleep peacefully every night. We are each other's number-one fan and top priority. By being loyal to each other, we're role-modeling good behavior to our kids. Call it "trickle-down parenting." Joe and I show each other loyalty and respect, and the kids learn to be loyal and respectful people. We teach this by example. If the marriage is strong, the children feel secure and they thrive.

HONESTY

We are completely open, without fear. Unless you can communicate and vocalize your desires and feelings, how is your partner supposed to know? We tell the kids, "Use your words!" Husbands and wives should, too.

Saying to a man, "You should just know how I feel without my having to spell it out!" is even more insidious than "What about me?"-ing him to death. Marriage isn't a magic show. It's not a bar trick. Joe and I can't read each other's minds. Fortunately, we don't have to. We both speak fluent English—with a little Italian thrown in.

Honesty can be flattering or instructive. It can also be brutal. When a man asks his wife to dress better or lose a few pounds, it can seem rude. I don't take comments like that as insults. Honesty is always a compliment. When Joe speaks his truth, he's giving me credit that I'm secure enough in myself to take constructive criticism. When Joe says he doesn't like my outfit, I know it's just because he loves seeing me in his favorite red shirt. If you respond to honesty with anger and defensiveness, your man will shut down. He might stop saying things— but believe me, he's sure thinking them.

In my marriage, I always want to know what Joe thinks. There should be no secrets between us. Fortunately, Joe is incapable of not expressing himself, critically, or approvingly. If I put on a dress he likes, he'll say, "You're the hottest woman in the world. Look at that ass. I'm having a moment!"

"Down, Tarzan!" I'll tell him to shut up and laugh. But I'm glowing and feel like I could take on the world. That's the power of honest praise.

Honesty is a two-way street. When I make a correction to Joe, I speak softly, and look him in the eye so he knows my words are coming from a loving place. Joe relies on me to say how I really feel. If you're always poised to jump down your spouse's throat over a perceived insult, insults are all you'll hear. But if you take each other words at face value, all you hear is love.

PASSION

You shouldn't marry if you aren't sexually attracted to your husband. Most couples are hot for each other on their wedding day. The cooling off comes a few years later. It is crucial not to let that happen. A cold bed turns into cold hearts. In an Italian marriage, you work hard, play hard, fight hard, and love hard. On the list of the most important things, we put sex one notch below food. Food is life sustaining; sex is marriage sustaining. I never let my husband go hungry.

Joe and I do it every other night, on average. Granted, enthusiasm varies. We have our epic mind-blowing sessions. But, in every relationship, boring sex sometimes happens. Doesn't matter. Sex is the glue of marriage. It fills in the little cracks to hold you together. Otherwise, those tiny cracks can turn into huge splits. Sex is how we bond emotionally, have fun, and burn off stress and release tension. (Or, as Joe says, "Get the poison out.") We're paying each other attention in a way no one else can. Our passion and chemistry are unique in the whole world because we are. Even when it's just okay, our sex is special.

So, there you have it. *Respect, Loyalty, Honesty,* and *Passion.* The four cornerstones of our home.

You might be thinking, *She forgot some major stuff on this marriage blueprint. What about Love and Trust?*

Love and Trust are the very paper the blueprint is drawn on. If the love and trust are frayed and torn on the edges, you can restore those sentiments with Respect, Loyalty, Honesty, and

Passion. Even shattered trust can be pieced back together. Love on the skids can be steadied and turned around. It might take some time, but it can be done.

Some marriages can't, and shouldn't, be fixed. In a bad situation, with abuse or cheating or lying, divorce might be the right way to go. But, if you started out in love and feel lost, I can help you find your way back home. If your marriage is just okay, I can get you to great. If your marriage is good, I can get you to amazing. When your relationship is as strong as a house, you'll feel that strength and confidence in yourself, and can follow your dreams through the roof.

In *Love Italian Style*, I'll tell the whole, juicy story of our life together, the secrets of how I keep it sexy and real, and how pleasing my husband influences every other aspect of our lives, from parenting to fame, cooking to singing, getting dressed to going out. Marriage is one subject that inspires and frustrates us all. To that end, I want to offer readers the lessons I've learned along the way. You can take my advice or leave it. But I believe that couples who "Gorganize" their marriages will strengthen the bond between husband and wife, and amp up the passion. A marriage based on mutual respect, honest, loyalty, and trust is as sexy and passionate as it is warm and loving. Despite the pressure of life in the spotlight, Joe and I managed to make it work and look easy.

I wish it were! Marriage is *hard*. I work at it every day. During our nine years together, we've had plenty of rocky times and major fights. Through it all, I stayed true to myself while trying to be the wife Joe wants. Readers might be shocked to learn that I do ninety percent of the housekeeping. I greet Joe at the door with a kiss, and make a hot dinner for him nearly every night. I uphold old-school Italian values, but I combine them with a modern lifestyle to follow my dreams. My old-meets-new approach seems to be working. My marriage is as passionate as ever. My kids are happy and healthy. My singing career is more than I could have ever dreamed of. Thank you, Jesus! And thank you, Joe! None of it would be possible without Joe's love and support. Our relationship is the center of our worlds. And, it's the focus of this book.

PART ONE

· ·

The Wilderness

I call this part of my life the Wilderness because I did a lot of my emotional wandering during those years. I also wandered up and down the East Coast, and lived in a handful of different houses and apartments. With the exception of my childhood home in Toms River, I never felt settled in those places. And even the house I grew up in, I associate with unsettled feelings.

Don't take "wilderness" literally. The closest I get to that is when a baby bear wanders into my driveway in Montville! I'm a city girl, always have been. Obviously, no one is going to call the East Coast of America an untamed wild (well, maybe parts of the Jersey Shore and South Beach . . .). But, until I met Joe, I did feel like I didn't know which way was up or where I was going. I totally related to the line in the old Madonna song, "I made it through the Wilderness. Somehow I made it through. I didn't know how lost I was until I found you."

CHAPTER ONE

· ·

The First Man in My Life

It's no joke that I married my father. Anthony Marco was, like Joe Gorga, a Leo, in the construction business, Italian, and from Jersey. He and my mother raised my two sisters and me in a comfortable house in Toms River. My father's job was investing in properties, and building and selling them. We were the first family to get a Lincoln Town Car on our block, in 1989. I'll never forget the Christmas that my father surprised my mother with his and hers Rolex watches. I thought it was so sweet and romantic. We always had new clothes, plenty of food to eat, and some luxuries. But I wasn't born with a silver spoon in my mouth by any stretch of the imagination.

People used to ask me all the time if I'm half black. My mother had no idea what to do with my hair. Did she own a brush?

My parents got together when they were seventeen years old, and kept that teenage, obsessive love going for all their years together. Anthony was Donna's one and only, her first and only. They had a traditional marriage. He went to work, and she stayed home with the three girls. My sisters Kim and Lysa were ten and twelve years older than me. I was the baby, their doll. They'd dress me up and play with my hair. I'd stand on the coffee table in the living room and sing. My father loved it when I sang, and always broke out the Camcorder to make a video. By the time I was eight, my sisters were eighteen and twenty. I always felt like I had three moms. My mother and father treated me like an only child. I was their baby, and they fussed over me.

With my sister Kim, one of my three Moms.

This idyllic life came crashing down when I was a freshman in high school. I tried out for the freshman cheerleading squad. The coach posted the final list, and my name wasn't there. All my friends were on it, though. I was devastated. I congratulated them, and they took pity on me.

Then, the coach put up the final list for varsity. My name was up there. I was as shocked as everyone else. This was unheard of, for a freshman to make varsity. My friends—so consoling when they thought I'd been cut from the freshman squad—were now sharpening their claws.

The older girls on varsity hated me, too. They screamed at me, pulled my hair, threatened me in the locker room and humiliated me in public. The school mascot was a pirate. They forced me to wear the smelly ridiculous pirate costume and run around the field all season.

I know, I know. First-world white girl problems. "The cheerleaders were mean to me!" story might not trigger much sympathy. The hazing was relatively mild. They didn't cut me, or put me in the hospital. But they did humiliate and torment me for no apparent reason. I hadn't done or said a thing to any of them, and yet they despised me with blazing irrational fury. The cheerleaders were my teammates. They were supposed to have my back. Instead, they were behind it, with knives. The rejection stung.

The cheerleader thumping, however, was a mere taste of what was to come. When I was a junior, my parents decided to move to Boca Raton. I was thrilled when I heard the news. I spontaneously broke out into a cheer. Gimme an F! Gimme an L! Gimme an O . . . you get the idea. I didn't know much about Florida, but any change would be *great*. And, year-round sunshine was a bonus.

Day one at Boca High, my new classmates sized me up as a freak. I had curves and wore a jean jacket. My dark skin and hair were marks of the devil to the pastel-draped skinny blue-eyed blond Florida girls. They viciously mocked my accent (can't say I blame them). The boys, meanwhile, were licking their chops and telling me how exotic I looked.

According to the Boca Bitches, my being Italian and from up North could mean only one thing: I was a slut. The opposite was true. I hadn't so much as kissed a boy. In Jersey, I was considered a prude. I bit my lip and put on a brave front no matter what was said about me, and waited for things to change.

About a month into the school year, one of the Boca Bitches called me at home. "Hey, Melissa. We want to take you to a party," she said.

I was psyched. *Finally, they like me,* I thought. Poor gullible, needy me. If I could go back in time to that phone conversation, I'd smack myself in the head and say, *Don't trust her!* Instead, in my excitement, I volunteered to drive her and two other girls to the party.

They said the party was outdoors in a neighboring town. I had no idea where it was, or where I was driving. I was new to the area and it was pitch black out. I just followed their directions.

"This is it," said the leader of the pack. I pulled into a driveway. We all hopped out of the car. As quickly as I thought I had "arrived," instantly, thirty girls surrounded me. *What the . . .* I turned to ask the girls who had invited me, and they looked back at me with a blank stare.

These girls wasted no time. One quickly rushed up to me and punched me. Bam. Full force, right in the nose. Instantly, it started bleeding.

I was so shocked, it didn't even hurt at first. About an hour later, my nose started throbbing and didn't stop for days.

This maniac girl rubbed her knuckles and accused me of sleeping with her boyfriend. I barely knew the kid. We'd spoken two words to each other. When did saying "Hey" to a guy in the hallway mean that you were having sex with him?

"I'm a virgin," I said to defend myself. It was the embarrassing truth. Yes, despite growing up at the corner of Whore and Skank Streets, or so they thought, I hadn't done the deed. Not even close. The girl didn't care. She already made up in her mind that I was to blame for her problems, even though I'd done nothing but be nice. (An interesting foreshadowing, as seen on RHONJ.)

The thirty girls were now slamming their fists on the roof of the car. It was like a scene from a gang movie that ended with me slumped and alone in the car. Desperate to flee, I hopped back in and started tapping the gas, hoping the girls would move out of the way. But they kept beating on the roof, the hood and the doors.

Fearing for my life, I stepped harder on the gas, making the car lurch forward. They finally cleared a path, and I floored it—right into a dead end. I had to turn around and drive through the pack again. This time, they threw rocks at me as I sped by.

Crying hysterically, I could barely see as I drove. It was a miracle I found my way home at all without crashing. My mother was horrified when I burst through the door with a bloody nose and red swollen eyes. When I finally stopped sobbing, I begged her to take me back to Toms River. I'd seen enough of the South to last the rest of my life.

My mother got on the phone to call my father. He'd stayed back in New Jersey, tying up loose ends. She told him what happened. He said, "Look, I'll be finished with my business in a month. Just hang on until I get down there."

A total Daddy's girl, I was instantly comforted. As soon as he arrived, he'd protect me and make it better. He'd keep me safe. No one would mess with me then. I sniffed back my tears. One month seemed like an eternity to wait for him. But I knew it wasn't really that long. I stayed focused on how incredible it would be when he finally walked through the door. I'd throw my arms around him, and never let go.

I counted the days, which made the wait harder and easier at the same time. I turned seventeen during that month, on March 21. Traditionally, my father bought me jewelry for my birthday gift. I don't know why, but that year, he sent me a card. I remember thinking, *This is weird*. He'd never given me a card just from him. Usually, a card was attached to my gift, and signed by both of my parents. As weird as it seemed, I loved it and immediately called him to thank him. "Daddy, I love my card. Thank you so much. It means the world to me." His handwritten note read as follows: "Melissa: Even though you are growing up, you will always be my little girl. And, no matter what, I will always love you and be there for you *no matter what*. I will always love my baby girl. Love, Daddy." Thank God I didn't pull a classic seventeen-year-old move, and toss the card. I still have it, in fact. It was as if I knew I should keep it and my father knew he had to tell me something and make it tangible for me to hold onto.

Eight days later, on March 29, I was at my girlfriend's house for a sleepover. My mother called very late at night on the phone. She was screaming and crying. "Melissa, your father was in an accident. He hit a tree and he died," she said. I dropped to my knees, and started howling. I threw the phone.

My friend asked, "What's going on? Are you okay?"

I couldn't speak. I was in complete shock.

My aunt came to pick me up, and brought me back to my house. My grandmother and uncles were there. My mom was in the corner crying. We booked flights back to New Jersey. Tissues were everywhere, everyone in a panic. It was a sad scene.

My mother had been alone when she got the news. I pieced the story together later on. It was a rainy night. He was driving around a corner, and hit a tree. He died alone on the road. He was only forty-nine years old.

> Melissa
> Even thoow you'll
> growing up you will always
> be my little Girl. And no
> matter what I will always
> love you, And be there if you
> need me. _no_ matter what.
>
> You're a wonderful daughter,
> and you deserve to hear that
> more than I tell you,
> because you're more special
> than words could ever say.
>
> Happy Birthday
>
> I'll always love my
> baby girl.
> Daddy.

The last contact with my father.

It took me a while to believe it. The shock knocked me out of my body. I felt like I was standing next to myself, looking with sadness at the girl who just lost her father. The trouble I'd had with the mean girls, which I had thought were huge problems, shrank to the size of a grain of sand. I did not know what pain really felt like until that moment. And, it got much worse as the days wore on.

Every morning was painful. When I opened my eyes, I wanted to immediately shut them again. I prayed that it was all a bad dream, that I would wake up and my father would still be alive. I remember going back and forth between feelings of complete and utter despair and terrible anger. There were many times I wished I could scream at him and ask him why he didn't have his seat belt on. If he would have had it on, he could have met my children today. It was hard not to be angry at him, but I missed him so much that most of my days were filled with tears.

In the fog of grief, my mother and I found out that we were dead broke. All of my father's money was tied up in the properties that he had bought to develop. After he died, the men he was in business with continued it and paid us nothing. Since the business was done on handshakes, not contracts, my Mother had no proof of my father's investments. They refused to give us a penny. There was no life insurance. No college fund. Hardly any savings. All we had in the world was our possessions, still in boxes on the floor of our Florida rental.

In an instant, the half a second that wheels spun out of control on the wet pavement, I lost my father and my future. My mother was equally devastated. She had been with my father since she was seventeen years old. She did not know a life without him. Nor did my sisters and I. Every next move we made seemed like walking in quicksand. Even breathing was hard. He was our anchor. We did our best to comfort each other, but we were overwhelmed. I must have radiated misery. Even the Boca Bitches took pity on me and left me alone. By then, it didn't matter what they said or did. I wouldn't have felt it anyway. Grief was my only emotion. A hole had replaced my heart.

I wanted all my memories of my father to be the good ones. I replayed over in over in my head the many times he took me to the Jersey Shore and put me on rides on the boardwalk over and over again. And, all the times he would take out his big Camcorder and video tape me singing and dancing on my living room table. He always told me I was his star. I will never forget the 34-foot Silverton boat that we spent so many weekends on. I can still see the bold rose-colored script on the back of the boat. He named it: *My 4 Girls*.

At the funeral in New Jersey, my father's brother and my godfather, Uncle Johnny, gave me a tight hug. He said, "You have a great future ahead of you, Melissa. I won't let this tragedy ruin your life. I'm your godfather. It's my responsibility to step up. I'm going to help you go to college." I heard his words, and appreciated his offer. It was a long time before I could wade through my depression and accept it.

We went back to Florida. My Mother had some prior experience in nursing, and she got a job to support us.

At this time in my life, I kind of rebelled. One day, my friend and I were out shopping. I put on a $19 sweater at a store. Even though I had enough money to cover it in my wallet, I walked out with the sweater on. The store clerk busted me. He pulled me into the back room and called my mother. She was furious, but she also understood that I was a little out of control then after my father's death. We got a court date. The judge asked us to pay a fine and the shoplifting charge was expunged.

I also made some rocky choices about men. I was attracted to the bad boys. I had this urge to control them and turn them into something good. My OCD kicked in, and I wouldn't let up until they'd transformed. My bad boys were like my own personal sociology project. By sheer force of will, I wanted to change them into nicer, sober, non-cheating non-douche bags. Yes, I had crazy love-hate relationships. The "I can't live without you, I can't stand the sight of you!" type that define the young, stupid era of life. You have to go through that period to know what you don't want, and definitely the kind of man you would *never* marry. The man I did choose to marry was the exact opposite. My bad boy projects failed. Assholes don't change. If I had known that at eighteen, I'm sure I would have made a lot of different choices about the men I hung out with.

I pushed on, too, and made it through my classes. Most of my emotional energy went into my schoolwork and my mother. Eventually I was accepted into a four-year college in Jersey City to study elementary school education. A pinhole of light penetrated the fog of grief. I was moving on. I would have a future.

True to his word, Uncle Johnny, God bless him, helped with tuition. I found an apartment with roommates and worked three jobs while attending classes in order to pay the rent. I might have started out the spoiled baby of the family, but any bratty sense of entitlement was gone. I was my own woman now. I had only myself to fall back on.

I was envious of girls with daddies to turn to. They could make a call, and their fathers would swoop in to fix their car brakes, give them a loan, or make them feel treasured and special. I missed that closeness. I found myself drawn to a certain kind of man, a father figure who made me feel protected and would tell me right from wrong. They weren't older than me per se. It was the authoritative and instructive personality type—someone who could take charge—that attracted me. I know a lot of women wouldn't like that. But I responded to it.

Between work and school, though, I didn't date a lot. Oh, I managed to kiss my share of frogs along the way. But no one guy held my trust. My goal was to become an elementary school teacher. Without family money or a business to fall back on, I was responsible for my own livelihood. Losing my father made me realize that you can't rely on a man to take care of you. You have no idea what might happen down the road. He might toss you over for another woman. He might bust out. Or, as I knew only too well, you could turnaround, and he'd be gone. I vowed that that would not happen to me. I was not going to put my security in the hands of a man.

When I went to college in Jersey, it felt like a fresh start. Despite my desire to connect, I had only one "serious" boyfriend during college. Looking back, it's laughable to call it serious. I didn't know what "serious" really meant in terms of commitment and intention until I met Joe. Neither did that boyfriend! He cheated on me.

It seemed like I met *only* frogs for a long time. No princes. I always held onto a glimmer of hope though. I'd been raised to be independent and a realist, and although I knew that fairy tales and unicorns didn't exist, I held onto a vision of what a great love could be. I was in love with the idea of being in love. For all its flaws, my parents' marriage was based on mad passion and deep-seeded love. I wanted that intensity—but only the best parts of it—for myself. I wanted to feel swept away.

I looked for potential in a thousand faces. If I noticed something in a man's eyes or smile, I'd test my feelings. I kept it fun and light. Yeah, I was a bit of a flirt. But there never seemed to be a real spark or true connection. Reality could never measure up to my fantasy vision of what love should be.

Besides, the men I met didn't want what I was offering. They were after hookups and one-night stands. I was only interested in a long-term romance. At parties and clubs, if a guy hit on me hoping for a one-and-done, he found out, but quick, that he'd get nowhere with me. If I went on a first date with him, I'd keep the conversation rolling, but I'd size him up in my head. Could this man be my future husband? What would our babies look like? How about his relationship with his mother? Close and affectionate, or *too* close and creepy? The mental checklist took the length of an average meal to get through. But usually, by the end of a single glass of wine, I knew if he'd get a second date. Just a handful of men did. It just seemed like a waste of my time—time away from studying and working to pay my rent—to go out with a man I knew I didn't want to marry. Only the fairy-tale romance would do. If you can't get through one date with a man, you're certainly not going to spend the rest of your life with him.

Clubbing in 1997. Blame it on Britney. It was all about the bare midriff.

On the weekends, my girlfriends and I used to go into New York City. Jersey City/Bayonne is only a few miles away from Manhattan. I'd save up all week long to go dancing on Saturday nights. I loved it. Every part about it. Most of all, planning my outfits. I was always into fashion. I tried every look out there. We would always go to the club that was the "spot"—sometimes the Limelight, the Sound Factory, or the Tunnel—whichever club had the longest line that was wrapped around two city blocks, we were at it. We would walk right up to the red velvet ropes, past the line, and somehow manage to maneuver our way in.

We were pretty and young, having a great time, and men flocked around us. At first, they flirted and treated me like a possibility. But then, after only a few minutes of talking, they'd say, "You're a girlfriend type." I had that air about me. Maybe it was because I was sober and not dressed like a slut. The message was loud and clear. Guys instinctively knew that if they wanted to get lucky, it wasn't going to be with me.

I'll never forget, this one guy said, "You might as well have 'Wifey' tattooed on your forehead. Why are you even here?"

Strange question. Why does anyone go to a club? I said, "I love music and love to dance."

He laughed and gave me a patronizing pat on the shoulder. "You should go home."

I wasn't playing hard to get. I *was* hard to get—nearly impossible.

Why so careful about men? I had my reasons. There was the other half of the story that I have not yet told about my father. It's very hard to tell it. I wasn't sure that I would be able to do so in this book. It is just so personal, and for many years, I buried any negative memory of my father. It didn't seem right to think about the bad. I did not want to remember him like that. He was so good, and I felt guilty tainting his memory with the hard truth. But I realized that if I do not tell the whole story, then I'm not telling the whole truth and my relationship with

In the Wilderness, in leopard print.

Joe won't make complete sense. I want all of you to know my true experiences (even the ones that are extremely painful to share), because I do believe they have molded me into the wife I am today.

I heard someone say once that the story of your death was the story of your life. My father died driving in the middle of the night on personal business that my mother and I knew nothing about. He died suddenly, like he had disappeared. He left us alone, afraid, confused, and devastated. The fact is, my father had left us alone and afraid before. He had disappeared before. Many, many times.

Anthony was a man of his time, his generation, and his circumstances. Nowadays, high school sweethearts, however obsessive they are with each other, usually go their separate ways after graduation. They go off to colleges to see how their relationship holds up with a little distance between them. Well, in South Jersey in the mid-1960s, most of the kids didn't go off to college. They didn't have a sense of a bigger world out there, or unlimited possibilities. If they were madly in love, like my parents were with each other, they got married, moved into a starter house or in with her parents, and began making babies.

My parents' mad love swept them into marriage at eighteen. That passion never waned, throughout their twenty-seven years of marriage. They graduated high school, got married, and she got pregnant. Within two years, my sisters were born. By the time my mother was twenty, her own childhood was miles behind her in the rearview mirror. She was a kid. Then, she blinked, and she was a grown woman with two babies.

My parents were both raised with the strong Italian Catholic beliefs that marriage is forever. No matter what went on between a husband and wife, it was their obligation and responsibility to forgive and forget, especially if children were involved. Sometimes, my father tried my mother's ability to forgive. He tried her strength as a wife and as a woman. In my memory, he's a huge presence, like my own personal hero. But I also remember him as a human being with flaws.

Like all young men, my father liked to party. But, he didn't want to do it with his wife. A wife was supposed to stay home, care for the kids and make dinner. A good woman didn't run wild. So, when the urge to run wild hit my father, he went elsewhere to chase it.

As young as six or seven years old, I remember nights and

days of anxiety, of not knowing or understanding what was going on. Dad was home, and then he was gone. Mom fretted and cried. She called her sister and talked, upset, panicking. I was mainly confused. *Where is he?* I thought. *He can't* still *be at the store getting milk.*

He'd always come home, after a day or a weekend. Or a week. His homecoming, for me, was a disquieting combination of relief and terror. My mother's tears would turn into anger. I have seen hairbrushes fly across the room, coffee tables cleared with the sweep of an arm. When it was over, both my parents would apologize to me. My father would sit me down on the couch, hug me and say, "You know Daddy loves you. It's okay. Don't worry. I just went to work for a while. I'm home now." My mother would watch with her lips tight. As angry as she was at him, she would never drive a wedge between my father and me.

Even as a child, I understood the bargain she made with him, and with me. To keep our family whole and together, to

Family portrait, 1986. Guidos in pastel.

make sure that her three daughters had a father to hug them on the couch and tell them everything would be okay, she would put up with his disappearances. Like all mothers, she made sacrifices and justifications for the sake of her kids. She chose her battles, and accepted the things she couldn't change.

A few times, my mother couldn't take one more minute stewing at home for my father to return. She told my sisters and I to throw clothes in our hampers, and we'd take them to my grandmother's house in the middle of the night. When we came home from those short stays, we'd find my father waiting for us in the living room. He'd hug us all super tight, kiss my mother, and we'd start over fresh.

Going to my grandmother's house was as far away as my mother would ever go. No matter what, she would never have left him. And he never, ever, ever, would have left her. Okay, he did leave the house. But he'd never leave the marriage. There was never a doubt that he would eventually return home to her.

My father was my only male role model. I didn't have any brothers. As a father, he was incredible, which on many levels made him a walking contradiction. He was very strict and impressed strong family values and morals upon my sisters and me. He wanted us to walk a straight line. And, we always did. We were not allowed to have boys call the house or walk to the mall without a reason or to buy something. He expected a lot from us, but he was always front and center at every play, concert, and cheerleading competition to support us. He was loving, strong, always in your corner, and would literally die for any one of us. He was a great provider and a great teacher. As a husband—not so great.

Adult children look back at their parents' marriage to define with they want—and don't want—in their relationships. What

I learned watching my parents' marriage was the value of loyalty. No woman was more loyal to my father than my mother. I learned that there is no pride in marriage, and that personal flaws and weaknesses have to be accepted on faith. I also learned that men aren't reliable. Even when you love them as hard as you can, they cannot always be trusted.

I have the utmost respect for my mother. She stayed with my father because that was what you did back then, but also because she was madly in love with him. Even if she had found the strength to make a change and get out of an unfaithful marriage, she would have stayed single afterwards. She used to say, "I have three girls. I wouldn't bring a strange man into the house. You'll always have your father." Until we lost him. He died when she was forty-seven. She cried over him for years. It tore my heart out to watch her sit on her bed and sob. After several years of that, my sisters and I pushed her to get out there and date. My sisters were both married with babies. I was in my twenties. She'd made enough sacrifices, and was still a young woman, in her early fifties. Finally, she agreed to try. Through mutual friends, she met Frankie. I was sitting in her kitchen when he came to pick her up for their first date. He wore big, bad crocodile boots, and drove her in his Caddie to Atlantic City for a night on the town. They had a good time, and that was that. Mom is not one for change. She met Frankie, dated him, liked him, and has basically been living with him ever since. They're devoted to each other.

Meanwhile, while my mother was getting back in the saddle with Frankie and finding love again, my focus was school and work. I always was a go-getter and never afraid of hard work. Life was happening, and I had goals.

I also prayed a lot. I had been raised religious, and grew up thanking God for my blessings. Despite my many conversations with God, though, I didn't feel a true connection with Him either. Praying often felt like I was talking to the ceiling. What was next for me? I felt unsure and afraid. I asked God again and again for comfort and guidance, but felt more confused than ever. Rudderless, I called a priest and met with him to discuss my doubts.

I said, "I want to thank God and believe that he hears me. When I pray, I don't feel a connection."

The priest said, "This is why it's called faith. Even if you don't feel a connection, you have to have faith that it's there. Don't worry about whether God hears you or approves of your prayers. Just speak to God from the heart. Use prayer to understand your own feelings."

I took his advice, and stopped worrying about whether God was listening. I searched my soul for my deepest desires, for what I wanted more than anything else in the world.

"Thank you, God, for my health and my family. For a strong body and mind," I said. "Please God, send me a good man. Someone who will make me feel safe. A man who would make me miss Daddy a little bit less. A man I'm attracted to, who is attracted to me. He doesn't have to be rich, but let him be a hard worker and have goals in life. Let him be a man who will fix my car brakes, and knows what it means to love unconditionally. Thank you, thank you, thank you. Amen."

I made the same prayer every night for two years.

And, then God sent me Joe Gorga.

CHAPTER TWO

. . . .

Enter Joe

Joe loves this story. One of the secrets of our marriage is to grant him his moments. I call them "Joements." Whenever you see bold type set in a box, like below, know that these are my man's words. For extra fun, read it out loud in Joe's voice.

Hey, ladies. It's me. The one and only Joe Gorga. I'm very proud of Melissa for writing this book. I'm honored she wants to hold up our marriage as an example for other woman. I knew she was the woman for me when I first laid my eyes on her.

Back in 2000, I went to Cancun for a spring break vacation with a bunch of my friends. At twenty-six, I was a little old for spring break, but I had been working full-time since I was eighteen, and never took the time off. I finally caved and took a trip. My boys and I were hanging out by the pool. I had a drink in each hand and a lady on each arm. I glanced across the pool—it was a big resort with hundreds of people around—and I saw this girl with the most amazing curly hair in a leopard print bikini with big Gucci sunglasses.

I turned to my buddy and said, "You see that girl in the leopard bikini and shades? She's going to be my wife."

He laughed. "Whatever you say."

Later that week, we ran into some of her crew at a club in downtown Cancun. We got to talking. Turns out, they were from New Jersey, too. "Where's the girl in the leopard bikini?" I asked one of them.

I wanted to get as much info on my future wife as possible. I found out that her name was Melissa, she was twenty-one and that she worked part-time as a bartender. When I returned home, I asked around, and quickly found out my dream girl worked at Joey's in Clifton, a famous nightclub in our area.

I wasn't much of a club guy. I'd been busting my ass in my business for years already. I grew out of clubbing early. But to see this girl again, I'd go.

Before I had the chance to make it into Joey's, I drove down to the shore one weekend with the boys to go to the Surf Club. As soon as I arrived, I started partying, looking around. And, much to my surprise, there she was. My dream girl. My future wife. Melissa walked right by me with her girl-friends. I was with another girl, but kept my eye on Melissa. She was straight-faced, almost poker-faced. She would give me a little smile, but that's all I got. Her body language said, "Keep 200 feet back." The whole summer went by, and I didn't talk to her at all.

During the winter, I was busy with business and with girls closer to home. I didn't forget about Melissa, though. She was always in the back of my mind. I'd been working on a big project. After months of planning, I finally got the green light from the city—all systems go. My attorney, architect, and I went out to celebrate at Joey's in Clifton. I walked right up to the bar.

Melissa was standing behind it.

She asked, "What can I get you?"

I was shocked to see her. I'd totally forgotten she worked there. I'd blown my chance to talk to her last summer. Not this time. "You're everything I want in a woman," I said. "I'll put you on a pedes-tal. Go out with me."

Melissa laughed in my face. She blew me off! I realized that the setting might not work to my advantage. She was a hot bartender, but not your usual type. Her focus was work and making money to put herself through college. Every guy who came in there hit on her on all night long. She shot them all down.

The thought made me suddenly protective of her. I wouldn't leave her bar all night. I kept buying drinks. I asked her out again. She turned me down. Again.

I went back the next week, and walked right up to the bar.

"What can I get you?" she asked.

"I can't stop thinking of you," I said. "I can't breathe. I couldn't wait to see you again!" She giggled a little. "Did you hear what I said?"

"Oh, I heard you," she said. "I've heard some things about you, too. You're a womanizer. You've been engaged twice."

The truth: I got engaged at twenty to my high school girlfriend. I stayed with her for ten years and wasn't faithful. After we broke our engagement, I had a run of flings with other women. But that was all behind me.

"I would love to take you out," I said. "Just one dinner."

"No, thanks."

I had to convince her to change her mind, and would stop at nothing. I found the girl who walked around the club selling flowers. I bought every rose she had. I piled them on top of the bar in front of Melissa. I asked her out again. "Come on. Come on," I said. "Please just one dinner."

She looked at me with those gorgeous eyes and said, "No, thank you. Not now."

What's a guy got to do? I've never had to beg for someone like this in my life.

I was hesitant to give him my number. I didn't want to set myself up for getting hurt, and I had heard that he was engaged before. I had major trust issues, and this guy was like a neon beer sign that flashed, "Stay Away!" He came off to me as one of those typical old-school Italians where it is his way or no way. The expression of shock and disbelief on his face when I turned him down said it all.

He *was* sexy, though. His eyes were intense. When Joe talked to me, his eyes were on my face, not my boobs. He didn't check me out in the typical way that most guys did. He seemed sincere, like he was trying to peer into my soul. His lips captivated me, too, and not only because he said so many funny things. I started to look forward to seeing Joe each weekend, and thinking about him. I told my sister Lysa what he'd done with the roses. She said, "Just go to one dinner. What's the big deal? It's not like you're going to marry him."

She had a point. I decided that the next time he came in, I would say yes if he asked me out.

But he didn't show up. Not that weekend, or the next.

It had been two weeks since I'd seen Melissa. I still thought about her every day. But I wasn't rushing back for another rejection.

A buddy of mine called me up. "Hey, Joe," he said. "You know that bartender at Joey's in Clifton? She was asking about you." He'd been there and talked to Melissa. She remembered seeing him with me. Apparently, she wanted to know when I was coming back. After blowing me off for weeks, now she wanted to see me? This girl was not used to being ignored.

My first instinct was to play it cool and make her wait. But I was too anxious. I jumped in my car, drove over there, and walked right up to the bar. We looked at each other and said, "Hi." Then she slid a cocktail napkin across the bar to me with her phone number on it. "Just one dinner," she said.

The next day, I called her and said, "I'm not going to take you out. I'm going to make you dinner at my house."

I called my sister back. "Listen to this. He wants to make me dinner."

"Just go."

I went. His house was very impressive. He brought me right to the dining room. The table was beautifully set with candlelight. The food was ready—penne à la vodka, veal, and a salad. He pointed to a bottle of Grey Goose on the bar and said, "I made the vodka sauce with that bottle."

Years later, after moving in with him, I realized that Joe had ordered the food from our favorite restaurant down the street. Penne à la vodka and veal would become a weekly dinner, and happy reminder of that first dinner. He had put the food in pots and pans to make it look like he cooked it himself. We still laugh about it.

On a tour of the house after the meal, he showed me a mural he'd had painted on the wall of his living room. "I'm going to have my artist paint your face on this wall," he said. He looked absolutely serious.

I thought, "This guy is nuts."

He was funny, though. And all his craziness was so different. I realized later I didn't run through my checklist in my head. I was in the moment with Joe, not seeing how he'd fit into my future.

I was *way* into her. We had a nice dinner, a great conversation, and a few drinks. I took her to the couch by the fireplace to have a glass of wine. We talked some more, and then I leaned in and gave her a kiss. It was soft and sexy. I pulled back to check her reaction.

She smiled and said, "Thanks for everything. You've been so sweet. I have class in the morning. I have to go."

I really did have class, and I was still a bit wary. I hadn't had a chance to go through my checklist. I had no idea if he warranted a second date on the standards that mattered to me. So I went out with him again. And again. And again. I'm not sure when the checklist got thrown out the window. It just didn't make any sense with Joe. Looking back, I now understand that the checklist was a construct I had made to justify blowing off all of those other guys. I needed a logical reason not to bother with them. With Joe, however, logic did not apply. I didn't have to ask myself if I could see him as my future husband. I knew he was. By the end of the month, we were a unit. Two people, one life.

> When I was 12 and she was 10
> We had a sister and knew it then
> That things would change, like never before
> We had a baby to love and adore.
>
> You went to college to see what you'd be
> And when you came out a graduate we see.
>
> You want to be a teacher, or so you say
> When that day comes we all will pray
> That kids will stand straight
> All in a line
> And then you'll come home
> And drink lots of wine.
>
> Now you no longer search
> For that fish in the sea
> You found your own Joey P.
> Inside Joey G.
>
> She now has a man to stand by her side
> A husband he'll be, to love and to guide.
>
> And Joe you can't go out after it's dark
> Cause God forbid if that dog should bark
> She'll run and she'll hide and she'll get on the phone
> And she'll cry and she'll scream
> **I CAN'T BE ALONE**
>
> And though our Dad's not here to see
> What a wonderful woman she's grown to be
> We're sure he's proud and smiling down
> Knowing that Joe's part of our family now.

A poem by my sisters about Joe.

THE 100 DATE RULE

· · · · · · · · · · · · · ·

Regarding when to get down and dirty, I keep my foot firmly on the brakes. I follow the 100-date rule. I'd rather my daughter Antonia didn't have sex at all until her wedding night. And, as far as she knows, I didn't either.

Joe and I waited a long, long time. It was a challenge. We were wildly attracted, and really young. We couldn't keep our hands off each other's fully clothed bodies. But we held off. It wasn't purposeful or manipulative. Having sex too soon was just not an option. A few nights, I stayed over at his house, and even slept in his bed next to him. Nothing happened. He didn't even try too hard. Joe didn't want to put me in the category of a one-night stand, so I think he was secretly relieved that I was not "easy." It took the pressure off of him. Even if sex with me turned out to be the greatest night of his life, he'd lose some respect for me in the morning. I'm not going to apologize about how unfair that sounds, how sexist or old-fashioned. The fact is, a man won't fall hard if a woman is too easy. It's as true today as it was thousands of years ago.

Some women think waiting to have sex is just a strategy women use to trick a man into marriage. The opposite! For one thing, a "trick" is what whores do. For another, having sex too soon changes the dynamic of the relationship. Suddenly, it's all about sex, and not about getting to know and respect each other—especially from the man's perspective. Romance turns into booty calls. Joe and I both wanted to draw out the romance for as long as possible.

After a few months of "not releasing his poison," Joe definitely tried harder to seduce me. He'd go for it, and I'd say, "No, no." As frustrated as it made both of us, he was grateful I took the responsibility of making our relationship pure. We finally did have sex *on our wedding night*—hey, that's my story and I'm sticking to it. (Antonia may read this book one day!) It was worth the wait.

It's like a math formula. For every date you wait, it will be that much more powerful when the time comes.

Joe and I got "serious" in record time. After a month together, we were attached at the hip. After six weeks, I went on a family vacation with the Gorgas to Punta Cana. That trip was incredible. We were at a gorgeous resort. I was in my Hawaiian Tropic days of slathering on baby oil and lying out on the beach. Joe and I were so new, and so crazy for each other, he made me feel comfortable. I wasn't a total nervous wreck, worrying about whether his family liked me—well maybe a little bit of a wreck. The pressure is always on when you are meeting your guy's family for the first time. Even if your guy's family is exactly like yours, same background and upbringing, there are always family dynamics at play, especially when it comes to an Italian mother and her son. I did my best. I smiled. I was polite and said, "Thank you" a million times. Joe and I were off in our own little new-love world, though. It was hard to break out of that. I don't know how his family felt about me after that trip. They certainly formed their opinions afterwards.

I was living with two roommates at the time in an apartment in Bayonne, New Jersey. My godfather Johnny was helping out with my college tuition, but I was paying for everything else, including the rent, toilet paper, food, hair products, car insurance. I had this cute four-door white Mercedes that needed a lot of care and worked three bartending jobs to cover my bills, as well as student teaching and substitute teaching. I've always had nice things, and worked hard for them. That was how I was raised. But that was not, apparently, how one of my roommates was raised.

I arrived home after the Punta Cana trip, and the apartment was empty. All the furniture I'd brought with me or bought for the place was gone—the leather couch, kitchen table, the pots and pans. One of my roommates had cleared the place out. She took the family pictures off the wall, and they weren't even her relatives! The nice way to put it is that she permanently borrowed my possessions without asking and never returned them. The true way to say it is that she was a thief and a criminal who stole all the things I busted my ass to buy.

I never saw her again. She vanished in the night like the mist. It was crazy. My other roommate and I were shocked. It was like that movie *Risky Business* when Tom Cruise left his fully furnished house for a few hours, and came home to dust bunnies and bent nails on the wall.

What can you do? You have to roll with life's punches. My roommate and I still had our mattresses to sleep on (we had to get new sheets, though). To top it all off, my only roommate standing told me that she was going to have to move out in two weeks, because she could no longer afford the rent if it was only the two of us splitting it. I went into overdrive looking for new roommates or another apartment.

When Joe caught wind of this, he was not having it. He immediately said, "Move in with me. I've got this big house. I'm never home. I know we're going to get married eventually, so why not?"

Joe was a strong personality, maybe a little crazy, but good crazy. We were relatively new to each other, but I'd met his family, friends, and his staff. I'd heard plenty about him before our first date on the Jersey gossip vine. He was safe. But what about the possibility of a breakup? My gut told me it wouldn't happen. And, I always follow my instincts. Despite my religious upbringing, I agreed to live in sin with Joe. It felt right. I didn't question it.

There was just one catch. I had a nine-pound Pomeranian named Gucci. He was my life. My baby. My world. My one true love before Joe. But Joe was not a "dog person." He had never had a dog in his life and did not want one in his house.

My first baby! Gucci and I having an intimate moment in 2000.

There was no way that I was moving in with Joe without my baby. Gucci and I came as a package.

So, my few remaining possessions, Gucci, and I moved into Joe's house in Franklin Lakes. I immediately started cleaning it to my standards. He learned something new about me right away: I'm kind of a neat freak. I'm OCD about dirt and things being out of place. If plates and shoes aren't put away properly, I feel edgy and have to fix them.

I'm addicted to straightening. Some people might find that annoying. He loved that about me. Joe is the same way. I would sometimes go a little overboard to the point of making sure that Gucci's food was perfectly centered in his bowl when I fed him. It couldn't be too far to the right or left of the bowl. It had to be exactly in the middle. Yes, I'm that bad. We just really like a clean house. We're proof that a couple can be obsessively clean, and also really dirty at the same time. And, the ironic ending to the story is that Joe came to love Gucci even more than I did. Joe and Gucci bonded, and for many years, he was the center of our family. Antonia got to meet Gucci and to this day, still cries that he is gone.

So even though we were saying "I love you" and Joe told me he wanted to marry me, the trust issues stemming from my father didn't let up. I would still get suspicious about Joe, despite his seemingly loyal behavior. But, then again, I'd think, *My father was loyal to my mother, too, at first. Can I really trust Joe?* I wanted to believe he was a good guy, but the distrust was deeply ingrained. If Joe said he was going out on a Sunday morning to do estimates on properties, I'd always question it in my mind. My father was a builder, too. He used to say the same things to my mother. And then we wouldn't see him until Tuesday.

"I'm going out. I'll be back later," Joe would say. I wouldn't hear the words, I'd only feel the anxiety.

Intellectually, I knew that my "to be" husband was not my father, but emotionally, I had to keep myself in check and not let my past determine my future. Joe was not my father. He was like him in many of the good ways, but thankfully, Joe did not have his flaws.

At first, Joe didn't understand my trust issues. He hadn't done anything shady to raise suspicion. "Why are you so worried about my going to work on a Sunday? You should be glad I'm working!" he would say.

I finally worked up the courage to reveal the whole truth to Joe. That day was a real turning point in our relationship. He already knew my father died in a car accident. Then, I told him the rest—his infidelities, disappearing acts, the distrust that lingered in my heart. My feelings about my father are so complicated. It's a thick stew of love, grief, and anger. The emotional scars aren't visible on the surface of my skin, but they run deep inside.

I'd never told another man so much about myself. I realized that the very act of confiding in Joe was a sign that I *did* trust him. I could really open up with him. If I could share my thoughts and feelings, including fears and resentments that I usually kept bottled up, then it was possible I could share everything with him. My life. A home. A family.

I'd been searching for potential in so many faces, for so long. And then, like a bolt of lightening, I could actually see it. I'd entered the relationship with Joe with zero expectations. And then I found my prince.

> You found me? Wait a minute. It's the other way around. I found you.

I'll give him credit for that. Joe believed in "us" way before I did.

When I talked from the heart, Joe listened. He looked right in my eyes. I could see him take it all in. Not once in this very intense talk did he belittle my feelings or tell me I was wrong to have them. And, in fact, part of what makes our relationship work is that Joe needs to hear affirmations from me, just as much as I like to hear them from him. We are very similar that way. We get each other.

THE LION AND THE RAM:
A WILD LOVE STORY

· · · · · · · · · · · · · ·

When I imagine a meeting between a lion and ram, it doesn't end well for the ram!

But we're not talking about the animals in the jungle here. I mean astrology, the zodiac. Like any twenty-four year old in a new relationship, I checked out our sun sign compatibility online at a few Web sites. Not saying I put so much stock in astrology, but who isn't curious about it? Even if you don't believe, it's fun to look.

As I quickly learned, Aries the ram and the Leo the lion are a perfect match, especially when the Aries is a woman (hello) and the Leo is a man. Ours is among the most fortunate out of hundreds of possible combinations. On the charts I found, our combo was symbolized with a giant throbbing heart, or a ball of fire. It's no surprise we got together. Apparently, an Aries woman and Leo man would zero in on each other in a packed room—or a crowded Cancun pool.

The Aries Woman . . .
Love to be admired
Strong and independent
Often feels vulnerable
Up for new challenges
Likes to get her own way
Energetic, lots of get-up-and-go
Extremely witty
The life of the party
The most mothering sign of all of the Zodiacs
Ready and eager to argue her point (Very me, especially the part about
    appearing strong but feeling vulnerable.)

The Leo Man . . .
King of the forest (and the castle!)
Hardworking and driven
Generous, warm, and loving
Loves to give; loves to get
Romantic and passionate
Needs to call the shots and be in charge

Possessive and protective
Strong, firey and sometimes has a temper
Needs to be respected and admired
(Is that not Joe to a T?)

Put the Ram and the Lion together, sparks (and teeth) fly.
The good news
Two fire signs in love have a burning passion.
They're in-sync with each other's thoughts and feelings.
They're so close, you can't fit a piece of paper between them.
They are both hard workers who'd bust their asses for each other.
They are driven to please each other, in and out of bed.

And the bad news
Two major egos will clash in an epic power struggle.
They are both competitive and want badly to "win."
Jealousy could strike a major blow to their intimacy.
It can be a struggle for Aries to let Leo be in charge. She'll have to
   push through solid brick walls to learn how to back down for the sake
   of their harmony.

When you read horoscopes, you tend to get excited and optimistic about the hopeful, flattering parts, and gloss over the negatives. When I read about Joe and me, I paid attention to the claims of burning passion and strong intimacy. I glossed over how we'd clash and have epic power struggles.

As it turned out, every single positive aspect the astrologers predicted about us was right on the money.

But, so was all the rough stuff, too.

CHAPTER THREE

· ·

Melissa Getting Married

For my twenty-fifth birthday, Joe treated me to a weekend at the Short Hills Hilton. Anyone from the tri-
state area knows the hotel. It's located across from the
JFK Parkway from the Short Hills Mall, the ultimate high-end
shopping center in the area. As a girl who loves to shop,

spending my quarter-life birthday weekend at a four–diamond rated luxury hotel, crawling distance from Neiman Marcus seemed like a fantastic idea! I knew Joe would want to spoil the hell out of me, and I was psyched to let him.

Since Joe had to work on Saturday, the plan was for me to go to Short Hills ahead of him and he'd find me later. When I checked in, the concierge told me that I had a full day beauty package reserved for me. It was Joe's first gift. I practically swooned when I walked into Eforea, the Hilton's salon. Candles, the smell of jasmine and cinnamon, warm lighting, the gentle gurgling of the indoor pool. Ahhh, heaven. I thought, *This is going to be the best birthday ever.* I changed into a soft thick white robe and sank gently into a pampering coma.

A rejuvenating facial. A revitalizing massage. A reinvigorationg scrub and a refreshing aromatherapy mani-pedi. Whatever "re" they had to offer, I got it. Did I want to get my hair and makeup done, too? they asked. I said, "Sure!" It was the first time I'd had a professional do my makeup, and I loved it. Good thing! Who knew that getting my makeup done would become a part of my daily life for filming and performing?

Toward the end of my day of beauty, Joe called and said he was running a bit late. "I made reservations at the hotel's steakhouse for dinner. When you're done, go to the room and change. I'll meet you at the restaurant at eight."

Of course, I was a little bummed he was going to be late. But, then again, it was hard to feel bad about anything after four straight hours of being rubbed and scrubbed and polished like a gem. Our reservation was in an hour or two. That still gave me time to get dressed pretty for Joe and my birthday dinner.

I went up to the room, opened the door, and there was Joe.

I was momentarily confused. Just ten minutes ago, he had said on the phone that he was only just leaving work. How did he get to Short Hills so fast?

I hadn't put the pieces of the puzzle together yet.

Joe was on his knees. Candles everywhere. Long stem red roses filled the room. A bottle of champagne chilled in a silver bucket.

Holy shit, I thought. The details added up to only one thing.

We'd been together for just five months at that point. I was in disbelief on one level, but I knew it made complete sense on another. Two seconds passed between my opening the door, seeing Joe and hearing what he had to say. The moment shines like crystal in my mind, and will last forever. Also, in my mental movie of this scene, I look really good. Thank you hair and makeup people!

"Will you marry me?" he asked.

Is this really happening? Yes, it was. It really was. I was getting engaged. I started giggling, crying, and laughing at the same time. I screamed, "Yes!" He got off his knee, gathered me up in his arms and kissed me.

He said, "I told you I'd put you on a pedestal. I meant it."

I know some people think that putting a woman on a pedestal means a man doesn't see her as a real human being. By rising her up, he's idolizing her, turning her into a Goddess. Right? But you know what? I love being put on a pedestal by my man. Because I put him on one, too. I treat Joe like the greatest thing that's ever happened to me. It's easy to do, because it's true. And, the truth is that Joe wouldn't feel like a man if he couldn't shower his woman with love and attention.

Oh, I forgot to mention the ring!

How could I forget that?

At some point after I accepted his proposal, he pulled a red velvet box out of his pocket, and opened it for me. A round diamond, over three carats, with trilliants on each side and set in platinum. Joe had picked it out himself. We'd never talked about rings or particular styles. I had never let on about what size and style of ring I wanted. He went with what he thought I'd like. Man, was he on target. I loved it.

I slipped it on my finger. Of course it fit perfectly. He'd measured my other rings for size. My man thinks of everything. The ring hasn't come off since. *Am I really getting married?*

At my bridal shower with my mother-in-law and my mother.

I kept asking myself. *I'm going to be a wife?* The girlfriend-type girl was getting a big promotion. It really did take a while for it to sink in. While I was driving, I'd position my hand on the steering wheel so I could see it. I had to make sure it was still there.

I started calling around to find the perfect place for our wedding. Most places I liked were booked at least two years out. I could not believe it. Would we have to wait that long to get married? Then, the phone rang. It was Macaluso's in Hawthorne, New Jersey. They had called me back to let me know that they had just had a cancellation. I could have the date, but it was soon, in August.

From engagement to wedding in five months? Oh, why *not*? It was five months between our first date and engagement. We might as well make it a tradition. So, there is was. The date was set for August 20, 2004.

Some things are just meant to be. Macaluso's is the perfect place for a big Italian wedding. It was famous for ridiculous amounts of food and the best cocktail hour in New Jersey. And, as you know, we don't do things small. We invited 250 guests, basically, everyone we knew. People kept on asking me how I was going to plan a wedding in five months, but to be honest, everything just fell perfectly into place.

The one part of the wedding that I knew would be tough was the traditional first dance between the bride and her father. We had planned it out, so that my brother-in-law, Joey P., my oldest sister Kim's husband, was going to dance with me. I've known him since I was eight, and love him to death. He was like a brother to me, and I was grateful to have him in my life,

Look at that train. And that tan! Why didn't someone tell me to stop after my third tanning session?

and to stand in for my father that night. The band played "One Sweet Day" by Mariah Carey. It was a bittersweet dance. It was the only sad moment at the party, but good sad. I didn't want to get married without acknowledging my father's absence.

This is going to sound corny, so brace yourself: Our wedding song was "Endless Love," sung by Mariah Carey. I know. I must have been going through a real Mariah phase. I still absolutely love that song. Whenever I hear it, it makes me smile.

Another fun part of the night: At midnight on August 21, it was Joe's thirtieth birthday. I had a huge birthday cake made for him, and when the clock struck twelve, we all sang "Happy Birthday." Everything was perfect.

Joe, the quintessential workaholic, only had five days for our honeymoon. He let me know that there was no way he could

Joe's thirtieth birthday cake, served right after the wedding.

take off more time than that. I understood and was very happy to do a quick trip to The Atlantis in the Bahamas. I will never forget the first time I called Joe, "My husband," or when the woman at the check-in desk said, "Welcome, Mr. and Mrs. Gorga." I felt complete.

We returned from our honeymoon, and Joe immediately launched himself back into work. I had just graduated college and started looking for a teaching job. I had quit all my part-time jobs and was excited to start my teaching career. The first interview I went on, I got the job! My own classroom of third graders. I was thrilled. Although Joe was very proud of me, he sat me down at the kitchen table and said, "I want you to follow your dreams and take this job if you really want it. But, what if we want to go on vacation? I don't want to have to ask your boss for permission for you to take days off. Come work at my office with me, so that we can build this business even bigger to-gether." Joe had a way with words. And, I knew he was right.

Making the most of our short honeymoon in the
Bahamas.

In the end, I was fine not taking the job. Something in my
heart said it would be better for us and our future family if Joe
and I put our hard-working efforts together.

But, in a blink of an eye, my whole life seemed so different.
Joe worked from 6:30 A.M. to 8:30 P.M., I was only at the office
from 9:00 to 5:00. I found myself spending a lot of time alone
in a big house. With more time on my hands, I got to know my
next-door neighbor, a sexy middle-aged Jewish lady. She was
incredibly well put together. In her forties, she was thin as a
rail, and her face was as shiny and tight as a twenty-five year
old's. She dressed beautifully, even to just hang out at home.

Lovebirds.

Hosting her newlywed neighbor for lunch was a good enough reason to break out her diamonds.

I loved having lunch with her. It was hilarious. She would always want to know every intimate detail about our marriage. Yes, I mean sex. She talked about sex like a porn director. All she did was make dirty jokes and innuendo, and go on and on about how crucial sex was to the health of a marriage. Her husband was a very lucky man!

As she walked me to the door that day, she said, "Melissa, I'm going to give you the only piece of advice you'll ever need."

Get monthly Botox shots? I thought.

"What's that?" I asked.

"'Be a lady in the parlor, a cook in the kitchen, and a puttana in the bedroom.' Live by it, and you'll have a happy husband, a happy marriage, and a happy life."

It was hysterical. I started laughing. She laughed, too, but insisted, "It's true! Make it your mantra."

I mentioned it to Joe later that night. He made a little correction: "Be a lady on the streets, and a freak in the sheets."

"What about 'cook in the kitchen?'"

"That, too."

"Maybe that should have been my wedding vows, instead of the quote from Corinthians." I said.

Can you imagine? The priest saying, "And will you, Melissa, be a lady in the parlor, a cook in the kitchen, and a whore in the bedroom, 'til death do you part?" It would have definitely made our guests sit up in their chairs!

Well, I made that vow to Joe in private, and have done my best to uphold it. It hasn't always been easy. But it's worked out pretty well for us.

Nine years later, I'm proud to say that I'm the best lady, cook, and puttana I can be. Always room for improvement, though. I aspire to be an *even better* lady, cook, and puttana in the future. And so should you!

(I'm kidding! But not really . . .)

THE FIVE-YEAR CONTRACT

My version of a pre-nup is a five-year contract, I wouldn't bother with all the details about dividing up dollars. Mine would have only one clause: The couple can't separate until five years are over, no matter how many fights they have, or how epic the power struggle between them. Based on my experience, it takes five cycles of four seasons to build the foundation of a marriage, meaning the solid structure of values and lifestyle decisions that have to be sorted out.

You might think you and your new husband can just sit

down with an iPad, and bang out your official policy on the biggies: money, parenting, housework, in-laws, vacations, control of the freakin' remote. You could promise each other on day one that you will always, for example, spend equal time with each other's families, or never bring work frustration home with you. But, on day 1,001 you'll realize that all those plans you made on the iPad aren't worth a dime. Until you live through the negotiations and bad patches, the hurt feelings and disappointments, you have no idea how the marriage operates. What winds up making you happy might be the exact opposite of what you thought. Or not. The point is, it takes trial and error to become a couple. You can talk about how you're going to be until blue in the face. But how you're "going to be" might be a far distance from how you actually are.

Life is messy. Marriage is messy. And it's always going to be messy. But if you have half a decade of history backing you up, you learn how to clean up those messes faster and better.

There were many times, and many fights, when I wondered if I could stay with our marriage. I was not going to be a doormat. No way. Around the three-year mark, I stopped feeling defensive and was able to see my marriage from a new perspective. My attitude shifted. By the five-year mark, Joe and I were totally in sync and incredible together, just like our horoscope said we would be. Of course, we still fight. But now, we know *how* to fight productively (more on that later) as well as how to smooth it over and make up. Now, we can rely on what we've learned about each other. We know what pushes each other's buttons, what to say, what not to say. It took a full five years to get there. Every time a new issue pops up, we get tested all over again (like being on a reality TV show; more on that later, too). If a couple bails on the marriage before they give it a real, solid five-year effort, they wouldn't know the profound happiness of having come out the other side and the deep love that comes from surviving hard times together.

Granted, some couples should break up, especially in abusive or unfaithful unions. But if there's real love, you can't give up too quickly. In our culture, we want everything to be perfect right away. But in a marriage, it doesn't work like that. It takes time to push past ideas and problems that limit the relationship. Those five years are a trial by fire. On the other side of the fire wall, there's deeper understanding, love, and trust. In fact, I'd say that if you can make it to five years, you can probably make it to fifty and beyond.

PART TWO

· ·

Lady in the Parlor

What is a lady? Someone who can hold her head up high. She knows how to dress for the occasion. She's courteous, respectful, which makes others treat her with courtesy and respect. Manners! A lady is gracious and says "thank you" and "you're welcome," chews with her mouth closed, puts her napkin in her lap, and doesn't clear the dishes until every person at the table has finished eating. Don't you hate it in restaurants when the waiters do that? I'm a slow eater, and I always feel rushed if I'm the only one with a plate in front of her.

A lady isn't necessarily stuffy, snobby, or so proper you're afraid to speak to her or feel turned off by her. Exactly the opposite. A lady is warm, kind, loving, compassionate, and makes you feel comfortable and significant. She's approachable, friendly, kind, polite; a stylish woman who carries herself with dignity and pride.

What's the parlor? In the old days, the parlor was the public room of the house, where guests and callers were "received" for tea and cakes. For me, the "parlor" represents the rooms I use to entertain in at home, but also any public place. That includes the street, a restaurant, the mall or a club, or on TV. Bravo is like the public parlor. And, we all know, I am not that private! Much of our marriage takes place in the public realm, either out on the town, entertaining in our home, or filming for television.

CHAPTER FOUR

Look the Part

As modern women, we have a million ways to take pride in ourselves. Some women take pride in their kids, their home, their careers, their charity work. I take pride in all of the above, and also in my appearance. It's not vanity to care about how you look, as long as you don't equate looking good with being a good person. Putting on an expensive dress doesn't make you rich in love. A great head of hair doesn't mean you have a great mind. In our looks-obsessed culture, it's a shortcut to put more effort into how you look rather than how you behave. That shortcut, however, takes you nowhere.

Nothing looks sexy on a bitch.

Not to say that the kindest, sweetest, woman on Earth is smoking hot in baggy sweats and matted hair. Some effort to be presentable must be made. To put in the time, money, and energy required for style and beauty, you need motivation. So, what's a damn good reason to spend time and money shopping for flattering clothes? Why bother sorting through dozens of shades to find the right lipstick? Because looking good makes you feel good. It's cliché, but very true. You get a boost of confidence.

Everything looks sexy when you've got confidence.

Confidence comes from within. Again, I know it sounds cliché, but these tried and true sayings really do have meaning. There is no way you can feel as good or as confident when you have hairy legs, are wearing no makeup and haven't been to a gym in weeks. When you put on your lip gloss, feel toned and healthy, and are wearing a pair of jeans that fit you like a glove, you are always going to feel more confident. For me, the cherry on top is Joe's praise. When he tells me I look hot, I feel like I can conquer the world. It's an indescribable feeling when your man says, "You're gorgeous! Look at you! You're the sexiest woman on the planet. Get over here!" You will glow. You'll pop when you walk. And he'll shine with pride having you on his arm. And, ladies, it's not about looks here, it's all about attitude.

> I love it when I walk into a room with Melissa and men stare at her. They all want her, but they can't have her. She's all mine!

Style and beauty know no size. Any woman can dress to please her man and herself, to feel sexy, right down to her undies—down to her *moisturizer*—if she follows a few rules about shopping, getting dressed, and wearing it well. I'm not going to give specific rules about what to buy. We all have different tastes, budgets, and bodies. But I have a few good strategies for using style to improve marriage.

I've divided this chapter into two parts: Style and Beauty. Style is everything you wear and how you wear it: clothes, jewelry, accessories, and shoes. Beauty is all the finishing touches, the buff and polish that takes your look to the next level: makeup, hair, and nails.

STYLE ITALIAN STYLE

Clothes have always been my thing. I love fashion—everything about it. From reading magazines to shopping to trying on to mixing and matching and going out on the town, I love it all. We all have our reasons and motivations for choosing what to wear. Our favorite clothes make us feel secure and attractive. Some women shop to look thinner. Some do it to look trendy. Some shop to impress their bosses or dates. I know most

A fashionista at three: All dressed up for Easter in a bonnet, ruffle socks, and my little white purse. Loved it all.

fashionistas don't dress to impress men. They dress to impress other women. Not me. I used to dress to please myself only. Now, I also dress for Joe. I feel the most attractive when I get positive feedback from him.

I definitely have a strong point of view when it comes to my style and what I like to wear. But, the one thing I've come to realize is that I need to take Joe into account when I get dressed. It's not just about me wearing the hottest trend of the season or the IT shoe. Part of looking good and feeling good is knowing that my man thinks I look sexy. Whenever I go shopping or get dressed, I always ask myself: Would Joe take one look at my outfit and try to rip my clothes off? Would he make me walk in front of him so he can stare at my ass? If so, then mission accomplished.

I always wear what I want and what I like, but I also aspire to be eye candy for my husband. If you want to, you can please your man without compromising what you love. Ladies, I'm not saying that it is the end all and that you have to wear only outfits that your husband loves. But you will feel the most attractive and sexy if you wear something he's into. I do. If you know you're going to be with him for the evening, then turn him on with the looks he likes.

So, my first rule of fashion is a gimme:

DRESS TO PLEASE YOUR MAN

Your husband married you for a reason. Remind him via fashion! Start by reminding yourself what he loves most about your body. Back when you first met, what did he compliment you on? Your boobs? Your butt? Legs? A tiny waist? Make sure your outfits emphasize that part. If he loves your waist, cinch it with a belt. Adores your boobs? Keyhole that cleavage.

DRESS TO PLEASE YOUR MAN, PART 2

Now, you might disagree with his opinion of your ass, for example. You might even want to hide it, and would much rather show off a part you love about yourself, like your pretty collarbone. Marriage is about making each other happy. So wear something that highlights both areas. A nice neckline for you, and a clingy skirt for him. A man doesn't look at his woman to get turned off. He looks to get turned *on*. He won't see what he doesn't like. He'll zero in on what he admires. And, if he loved your legs once, the potential is always there. If your thighs aren't what they used to be, then play up the ankle with a strappy sandal. Waist a bit thicker? Shop for a V-neck wrap dress. Or buy a top with a print that creates the illusion of a small waist. Boobs have fallen? Good news! They *can* get up, with a push-up bra. So what if you've gained weight? Dress the body you've got now. Look and feel great today. Yeah, it might take some effort and extra shopping trips, but it'll all pay off when your husband beams at the sight of you.

A KING DOES NOT WANT HIS QUEEN TO LOOK CHEAP

There is a way to dress sexy without looking like you're trying too hard. Show a little skin, but never too much. If you're going to rock a lot of leg, then cover the boobs, and vice versa. The only time you'll see me flashing acres of skin is when I'm at the beach or the pool in a bathing suit, when and where it's appropriate. It's never appropriate to wear a super-short mini dress with a boob-popping, midriff-baring tube top. Absolutely not. Even in my music videos, if I wear short shorts, my tummy is covered. I am very conscious of this. Joe loves to see my body in clothes, but with a degree of modesty. When a woman shows too much skin, her outfit sends the message that she's desperate for attention. "I'm insecure and overcompensating" is not the fashion statement that you want to make. Rule of thumb: when getting dressed, think sexy meets classy.

WAVE THAT FLAG!

Joe is a bull. When he sees red, his nostrils flare and he charges. I buy every red dress or shirt I see. I try to wear that color as much as possible, especially on our date nights without the kids. He says, "Oh, my God. You're gorgeous. I can't wait to get home." He knows that I wear red for him. It's the little things that count. It sets the mood for the night. Find out what color turns your man into a bull. Go shopping and wear it tonight. He'll appreciate it that you went out of your way and tried to wear his favorite color for him.

SPECIAL NIGHT = NEW OUTFIT

Part of what makes a special night is shopping for, buying, and debuting a new outfit. Who doesn't feel brand new in a new dress? Joe loves it when I surprise him with a sexy dress he hasn't seen before. It would be pushing the truth to say each time I put on a new dress, he sees me with new eyes. But a grain of that feeling is real. He can't take his eyes off me all night, and you know I can't complain about that.

LET IT SPARKLE

Nearly ever piece of jewelry I own was a gift from my husband or my Daddy. Joe has beautiful taste (thank you, Jesus), and picks pieces that fit my personality and size. Jewelry is one of the most special and sentimental gifts your husband can give. Even if he buys you a piece of jewelry that is not your exact taste, wear it for him. Trust me. It will grow on you. Just try it for a couple days. And, even if it doesn't grow on you, wear it on date nights for him, then put it in a drawer for your daughter or your son's wife. The best part about jewelry is that it is sentimental and an heirloom that will last forever. Just know if your man bought you a piece of jewelry, he put a lot of time into picking out the perfect piece for you. Just picture him staring at the jewelry case thinking about which one you would love the most. I hope the image of your guy shopping for you makes you smile. The two pieces of jewelry I wear every day are my engagement ring and wedding band because they represent my commitment to Joe and our love for each other.

This is one street that doesn't go both ways. If you notice, Joe never wears a wedding band. Joe has really chubby fingers (he will tell you so, too), and he thinks that a ring is the most uncomfortable thing ever. It used to bother me, but now I just tell myself that a wedding band is more of a chick magnet, kind of like a guy walking a cute dog or pushing a stroller.

LIFE'S EXTRAS

Accessories are baffling to men. Why have so many random pieces that could fall off or get lost? Men would take every accessory—sunglasses, headband, scarf, etc.—and wear them in a utility belt. (Can you tell I am married to someone that works in construction?!) Too many extras on an outfit do get in the way. With kids, they also get pulled off and played with. Since I had babies, every pair of sunglasses I've owned have been taken off my head with sticky hands and tried on small faces. The more things you have to worry about, the more worrying you do. I'd rather not. A hot handbag, a fly pair of shades (but, if you have kids, you may want to buy cheapies, they will get scratched!), a beach hat, a few skinny belts, and that's it. I let my clothes do the accessorizing for me. I love easy, statement outfits—one piece rompers or jumpers—put it on quickly, look hot and go!

LIFT OFF

Shoes! The queen of accessories. You can wear any inexpensive LBD (Little Black Dress) with killer heels and you're glammed up. I'm a crazy shoe addict. What can I say? It's my weakness. I call Jimmy Choo, Christian Louboutin, and Valentino three of my best friends. Whether a peep-toe platform or five-inch heel, they always lift me up and never let me down.

MY FASHION ADDICTIONS

· · · · · · · · · · · · · · ·

I love fashion so much, the list of brands is endless—everything from a Hanes tank top from Target to a fitted Chanel leather jacket. I love to mix and match. Everything you put on doesn't have to be designer or expensive. But, when I do go for the gold, I really do it up. Some of my favorite designers are: YSL, Dolce & Gabbana, Roberto Cavalli, Alice + Olivia, Haute Hippee, Valentino, Mandalay and, of course, my favorite, AG Jeans. When I surf the Web, my hit list includes: Net-A-Porter, shopbop.com, Barneys.com, shopambience.com, revboutique.com, neimanmarcus.com and singer22.com.

BEAUTY ITALIAN STYLE

As a teenager, I didn't go though a big makeup stage. I experimented a little. But I never left the house with a face full of makeup. I thought I looked like a clown with blush and bright blue eye shadow. Lip plumpers? They made my mouth burn. Foundation felt heavy and greasy on my face. I didn't need it anyway with my olive skin. I used to go to tanning salons and lay out in the sun with Hawaiian Tropic baby oil. That was my skin care. My five-minute face took five seconds. A swipe of mascara, a quick dab of lip gloss, and I was good to go. When I had kids, I was too busy doing mom stuff to worry about makeup. I didn't see what the big difference would be if I put it on anyway.

For big nights or family events, I tried to improve on the five-second face. I had no idea what I was doing in terms of technique. When I had my makeup done the night I got engaged, I loved the look. I tried to replicate it, but I was clueless.

Another five years went by before I had my makeup done by a professional again—for television interviews. Early on, while filming RHONJ, my routine was pretty much what I was used to: mascara, gloss, with some eyeliner. But then I started doing talk shows. I remember the first one I was on. As soon as I went into the greenroom, the hair and makeup girl started layering it on! I couldn't believe how much she slathered on my face. It was so thick, it felt like my face might crack.

I remember saying, "It's too heavy. That's not me."

She said, "When you're on TV, you need it to be exaggerated, or the lights will wash you out completely. Trust me. You need *more* of everything—foundation, eyeliner, blush, and lipstick—or the viewers won't see it."

When I watched the show later, I understood what she meant. What I thought looked crazy and overdone in the dressing room mirror actually came off as natural and pretty on TV. I was amazed. Honestly, that was the moment when I fell in love with makeup. It was the turning point that helped me understand how to create a polished look that looked good on TV and stage, that still felt comfortable to wear in my everyday life. The next day, I drove straight to the MAC store and stocked up with products. While the kids were at school, I spent the whole afternoon playing with them.

Okay, maybe I was a little obsessed. Can you blame me? My teenage crush on makeup came on like fever at age thirty. I had to catch up. But, as much as I tried to experiment with new makeup looks, I quickly realized that I needed to learn the tips and tricks of applying from a professional. I set out to find the best makeup artist in New Jersey. That's how I met George Miguel. He started working with me for appearances, photo shoots, concerts, and for RHONJ. I paid close attention and picked up his techniques, how he moved the brushes, the right brands, the best tones for my skin. Now I do my own makeup on weekends and during regular filming days.

Since everything I know I learned from him, I thought he should explain it here the same way he taught it to me. Drum roll please, here's . . . the one and only *George Miguel!*

When I first met Melissa, she didn't know what she was doing. She said, "I just curl my lashes, put on mascara, and gloss the hell out of my lips." I never leave home without my eyelash curler myself, so I was glad she considered curling a must. But otherwise, it was like teaching a baby to crawl.

I taught her a few things. The next time I came to see her, she'd done her own makeup. I took one look and said, "Oh, no! I've created a monster!"

A little knowledge is a dangerous thing! My early attempts were overzealous. I got better over time. At first, I experimented with different looks. Cat eyes, metallic shades, hot pink lipstick, mineral foundation—all the magazine trends. The majority of my experiments were a total waste of makeup. It was like taking armloads of clothes into a dressing room, and throwing ninety-five percent of it into the reject pile. But, then again, if you don't "try on" makeup looks, how can you find the ones that are right for you? It's a process.

With George's guidance, I developed a philosophy about beauty. I'd like to share it with you, along with the product

George, giving me lip.

details about my everyday makeup and my super glam tricks. First, some broad-stroke ideas from both of us (George is in *italics*; I'm normal type):

COMFORT COMES FIRST

Melissa loves to try all kinds of makeup looks. I'm all for new ideas and making adjustments. Women are inspired by what they see in magazines, movies, and on TV. Yes, the face is a blank canvas. Any woman can try any style, just like any woman can try on any dress. But it might not work for her. For real woman (non-models), the main goal is to enhance what she's got, and make her feel comfortable wearing it. If the look doesn't fit the woman, she won't feel comfortable.

BUT DON'T GET TOO COMFORTABLE

As soon as I get used to a look, I make a change. When you get stuck in a rut, you don't grow. Although you don't want to be a slave to trends, there's no harm in trying out the hot colors or styles of the season. I might sample ten new trends, and wind up adopting one or two. Right now, I'm obsessed with bronzy, goldy colors. They match my skin tone, give me a natural look, and I feel like I'm glowing.

BEAUTY IS EFFORTLESS

It's more attractive to see a girl on the go with just a touch on her lips and cheeks, than a woman with tons of makeup. That looks like she's trying too hard. I always prefer her to look light and effortless.

EFFORTLESS TAKES EFFORT!

It's like the old joke, that "natural" makeup takes ten products and an hour to achieve. The effort that goes into an effortless look is all the foundation building you do before the makeup goes on. It starts with eating healthy, exercising, getting fresh air, and inner calm. Otherwise, applying makeup really is, as the saying goes, like putting lipstick on a pig.

PICK A FEATURE, ANY FEATURE

If you draw attention to one part of the face, everything else should be in soft focus. With a big eye, tone down the lips. The same thing goes for a strong lip in hot pink or red. In that case, bring down the eyes and cheeks, keep the rest soft, or you'll look like a clown or a streetwalker. Just like an outfit with one statement piece, pick one feature to be the star of the face. People will look at you, and think, She's pretty, *and will feel attracted to you. But, if you play up two or more features, people don't know where to look. Their gaze darts all over the parts of your face. Instead of focusing in on your best feature, they'll feel overwhelmed, confused and distracted. All they see is makeup, not you. They think,* Too much gunk. *It repels people. Playing up just one feature lures them in.*

WHEN YOU CHOOSE A FEATURE, CHOOSE WELL

A lot of people think beauty is about hiding imperfections. Hiding a pimple is one thing. Generally, makeup is not plastic surgery (although George and I are the king and queen of contouring). Strategic blush application is not a nose job. Makeup's job is to accentuate the positive. Take your best feature, and run with it. If you have great lips, bold lip color is for you. If you have gorgeous eyes, do them up—glitter is your BFF (Hello! We all saw Season 4 reunion, right?!? I like to think that I started that trend! Wink! Wink!)

TREND ALERT

Beauty disasters happen when people see the season's makeup trends and try to incorporate all of them into their face at once. It would be like taking every fashion trend, and wearing them at the same time. Military jacket plus faux fur vest, plus colored jeans = fashion roadkill. Same with makeup. Try one beauty trend that suits your coloring and personality. Walk around all day with a dark lip, and see how that feels. If it doesn't sit right, forget it. With lips especially, the color trend wheel turns every season. A trend is an idea, not the law. Take the idea, twist it for your personality, and make the trend your own.

MEN HATE MAKEUP!

*Men always say how disgusted they are when they kiss a woman
and their faces come away slicked with makeup. To men, too much
makeup on a woman means she's trying to hide something. It reads
as false advertising. Joe Gorga prefers Melissa in no makeup at all.
He prefers Melissa in* nothing *at all! He's a very laid back guy about
beauty. Almost every time I am done doing Melissa's makeup, he
looks at her and says, "Ehhh, it's OK."*

MEN HATE SLOPPINESS, TOO

It's absolutely true that Joe says he'd love it if I walked around
with a naked face, and definitely a naked body! He's not one for
super flash or glam makeup or hair. But he does want me to
look clean, awake and polished, and that takes some product.
Before Joe comes home from work, I check my face. If I look
tired or blotchy, I put on some tinted cover, gloss, and mascara.
I don't do a full Loni Anderson, who used to wake up before
dawn to glaze her face, and rush to get back in bed so Burt
Reynolds would only see her camera-ready. But I do take those
ten seconds to freshen up a bit. I always feel better when I am
fresh faced. Don't you?

MY NUMBER ONE BEAUTY SECRET WEAPON IS . . .

Skin care! Respect is the foundation of marriage? Well, skin is
the foundation of beauty. Follow a daily routine with a cleanser,
moisturizer/sunscreen, and eye and night cream. It helps to
start early, in your teens. But any woman at any age can start a

skin care regimen and see improvement. Especially nowadays—the products out there are amazing!

MY MORNING ROUTINE

Every morning, I cleanse with Dr. Murad's Time Release Cleanser, and then three days per week, I follow up my wash with his Exfoliating Cleanser. And, always his Renewing Eye Cream. Lastly, I finish up with Dr. Murad's Pore and Line Minimizing Hydrater. I know it sounds like a lot, but when you keep all of your products lined up next to your toothbrush, it just becomes part of your everyday routine. Without it, you feel naked. After that, as George would say, my canvas is clean and hydrated.

MY NIGHT ROUTINE

It is never an easy task to remove all your eye makeup at night, but it's a must. If not, the result is clogged pores and styes. I don't think so. The best way to remove your eye makeup is with eye makeup remover pads. Forget the Kleenex or wadded up toilet paper. Believe me, I've tried everything. The little round pads that are presoaked in makeup remover solution are the best way to go. My brand of choice is Almay, and it can be picked up at any drugstore. To wash my face, it's back to Dr. Murad and his products. When I find a good thing, I stick with it. And, you should, too. There is always a lot of trial and error in finding the best skin care products for your skin. Keep trying until you get it right.

FACIALS

A good rule of thumb is to have a facial once a season for a fresh start. Try as you might, you can't dig out every blackhead or clogged pore with cleansers and scrubs. Having a professional do a deep cleaning and moisturizing treatment can't be beat. There are some things you simply can't do at home. Also, if you stick to the once-a-season routine, you won't forget to make climate-related adjustments to your skin care routine. In winter, switch to a richer moisturizer. In summer, change to one with extra SPF.

TANNING

My Hawaiian Tropic days are over. I don't tan. The opposite. I use sunscreen year-round. Since I quit tanning beds and laying out ten years ago, my skin tone is more even and less spotty. I still crave a tan, though, so I get sprayed. Airbrushing guarantees an even coat, as opposed to spray tanning booths. It's only logical. A person with an airbrush can be more precise than a machine. The price difference is negligible. When you get a spray tan for the first time, test with the lightest shade possible, especially before an event. You don't want to show up at a wedding looking like an orange. Come on ladies, you know the look I'm talking about—we have all seen that girl walk into the room, and everyone whispers, "Lay off that spray tan!" Most spray tans last five to seven days. For a sun-kissed glow during the summer, I usually rely on good old-fashioned sun by shore with lots of sun block on, of course. If I need a touch-up here and there or for an event or photo shoot, I go to the salon. In winter, I prefer a less tanned look. It seems unnatural to have a deep dark tan in Jersey in February. So, I mostly rely on my bronzers. My favorite is Nars in Laguna. I recommend it to all my girlfriends.

HYDRATE

Of course, expensive products do wonders for your skin. But you can make a major improvement with two products that are absolutely free: water and sweat. When I hydrate—eight glasses of filtered water a day—my skin glows. The saltiness in sweat is an all-natural scrub. A T-shirt–soaking workout also removes the impurities in your skin for a healthy glow. An older friend of mine started doing Bikram yoga, aka "hot yoga." She drank 50 ounces of water before each class, 32 ounces after, and sweat buckets during. I didn't see her for a few months. When we met for lunch, I was blown away. The difference in her skin was astonishing. She looked rosy, dewy, and at least ten years younger. The combination of hydration and sweating flushed out and scrubbed away her fine lines. Going to a 90-minute yoga class three times a week isn't as easy and simple as getting a facial. But, like marriage, healthy, happy skin takes work. If you put in the effort, you get the rewards. That's what I call "sweat equity."

BODY SHIMMER

Okay, ladies, this is my signature glam tip. It is a complete must. I *never* leave the house without some type of tinted, shimmering, body glow moisturizer, on your exposed body parts. If you have a sleeveless shirt on, lather up those arms; if you have a low-cut shirt on, make sure it is spread evenly on your upper chest, and if you are wearing a short skirt, go to town on those legs. It does amazing wonders for your skin. I always marvel at how it seems to hide every imperfection and gives your skin that healthy glow that both men and women drool over. It completely freshens up your entire look.

MY EVERYDAY MAKEUP

I keep it light, clean, and fresh.

- **Foundation.** A thin application of Laura Mercier tinted moisturizer.
- **Blush.** Just a tad. A couple of brush strokes of Nars bronzer or MAC blush in light pink or peach.
- **Eyes.** Usually something with a little light shimmer. And, always my beloved MAC eyeliner.
- **Lashes.** Curling is a daily ritual. George turned me on to L'Oreal Voluminous mascara. It's only about $6 at the drugstore, but it does an amazing job.
- **Lips.** MAC gloss or lipstick, usually in a pale pink or peach.

MY SUPER GLAM MAKEUP

Super Glam makeup is my game face for the red carpet and parties. When I've got glitter on my eyelids, you know I'm here to play.

- **Foundation.** When the eyes are set, move on to a light layer on the skin with Dermalogica tinted cover.
- **Blush.** Highlight the cheekbone, stroking upward to the hairline. We use Nars Orgasm. Remember—contour, contour, contour.
- **Lips.** Define them first with MAC whirl liner, and then MAC Cream Cup lipstick. For shine, we use MAC Love Nectar gloss on top of it all.

THE FAMOUS GLITTER EYE SHADOW

Melissa and I were testing this look for a while during the filming season and appearances, but we didn't go all the way until the Season 4 reunion show. She showed me the dress she picked out, a nude goddess dress with a Beyoncé/J.Lo glowy feeling, with embellishment on the top part along the shoulders. It only made sense to add glitter on her eyes to match the dress. The eye glitter would serve as a kind of accessory, so she didn't need a lot of jewelry. She wore earrings, one bracelet and a ring on each hand. When you do an eye this big, do them first, before the skin even. That way, if you get carried away with the eye, you won't have to tone down what you've already done.

HOW TO APPLY:
    Step 1: *Start with a primer. We use Urban Decay.*
    Step 2: *Stroke on a smoky brown and coppery shadow on the lid. On Melissa, we use MAC Rice Paper and Urban Decay Foxy. On the base of the eye up to the crease, we use MAC Saddle. On the crease, MAC Folie.*
    Step 3: *Wet the brush with water, and pat on the lid.*
    Step 4: *Dip the brush in glitter, and stamp it on the eyelid under the crease. Press it on. Don't swipe or drag the brush because you'll smear the*

> *eye shadow and the skin underneath will show through. We use Makeupforever glitter.*
>
> *Step 5: Repeat until the lid is covered with glitter.*
>
> *Step 6: Eyeliner. Melissa does the inside of her eyes to the water line, top and bottom.*
>
> *Step 7: Lashes! Curl, curl, curl. And, then mascara. Or, just go Super Duper Glam with faux lashes.*

THE BRAZILLIONAIRES CLUB

A few final words about hair and nails:

UP TOP

Listen, just make the best of what you are working with. There are so many products out there today to help you, from shiners to gloss to Keratin treatments to extensions. The list is endless. Thank you, Jesus. A woman's hairstyle is so personal that my only advice beyond finding the best style for your face is to make sure your hair always looks and *smells fresh and clean.* Guys are very sensory, so when they get close to you, they want take a nice inhale. (Smell is very important to Joe and me. I will get to that part later.)

DOWN THERE

I pose for photos in swimsuits a lot. Let me tell you, when you're in front of a camera in a string bikini bottom, you do NOT want to worry about a single hair out of place. I wax. Not all of it. Joe is a man and he likes me to look like a woman. A very well-groomed woman. One helpful hint, in my experiences with Brazilians: exfoliate well and often, or suffer the curse of the ingrown hairs. (FYI: Joe keeps his body hair under control, too. He's a dedicated manscaper. Chest, back, belly are kept hairless and clean. Other parts are also tended to. Not with a razor, but he gives himself a little buzz cut.)

HANDS

I subscribe to the 3 S's: short, shiny, and square. That's my motto when it comes to nails. I go back and forth between light pink and burgundy polish, and sometimes a French manicure. But I don't do 3-D nail art with inset rhinestones and dragon lady acrylic tips. I admire the artistry that goes into it. But, as a woman who cooks dinner most nights, my hands are constantly under water, or slicing tomatoes and chopping onions. Nine-inch nails would be a nuisance and a hazard. Risk a cougar nail falling off and landing in the lasagna? I'd rather die. If I came home with dagger metals tips, Joe wouldn't want me to go within fifty feet of his penis. And I couldn't blame him.

FEET

I get a pedicure at least once a month. During summer, twice a month. For colors, I usually match my hands to my feet. But, the most important reason why I get pedicures is because Joe and I love to rub feet at night before we fall asleep. It's part of our nighttime routine, and I definitely do not want to rub Joe's feet with sandpaper. Got to keep those peds soft and smooth. We all know Joe is into feet. He has had full-on make-out sessions with mine on national TV!

CHAPTER FIVE

• •

On the Town

An entire chapter about going out? The honest truth is that I'd rather stay home. By nature, I'm a homebody. My family is my life, and they're just about all I need to be happy. My very close friends that I've had forever are like family, so it's always great to have them and their families over. I keep my circle tight. Joe and I love being together with our friends and all of the kids. It just feels right.

If Joe and I do go out without the kids, it's usually together. In some of our friends' marriages, the husband and wife socialize separately. The women have lunches and girls' night out. The men go to bars and strip clubs with their boys. I think it's great for women and men to have their own friends and nights out with them. But I'm a strong believer that the couple that plays together, stays together. I'm not saying the guys shouldn't go to football games or play cards, or that the ladies can't have a spa day or a cocktail. Just make sure *most* of your nights out are together as a couple. I know some may think this is crazy, but trust me, it works.

So, what do our nights look like? Most weeknights are at home with the kids unless we have a work event to go to. Friday is almost always dinner out with Antonia, Gino, and Joey—usually just the five of us. Saturday nights the centerpiece of my weekend, are just for Joe and I. Whether alone or with our friends, my undivided attention is on Joe.

SATURDAY NIGHT FEVER

After a busy week of juggling Mommy stuff and work, I go all out. Super flash outfits. Super glam makeup. I want to wow Joe and make sure he feels proud to have me on his arm. The entire night, from getting dressed, to walking into the restaurant, eating dinner and having a drink, feels special and exciting, like when we were dating. We flirt, are on our best behavior, and, really enjoy each other. Date your husband, and he will always be your boyfriend.

DOUBLES DO'S AND DON'TS

Double dating with other couples that share your marital values makes your own marriage stronger. When Joe and I do it it's with fun-loving couples that enjoy each other's company. Hanging out with an unhappy couple that bickers and takes jabs at each other and wants you to take sides is uncomfortable and tense. As a friend, I would be glad to talk to the wife or husband separately to offer an ear or any asked-for advice. But on date night, I don't want to fend off their blows. I want to relax, have fun with Joe, and laugh.

SINGLES DO'S AND DON'TS

Listen, we all love to hang out with our single friends. Who's more fun? But, let's call a spade a spade. You can't make a habit of it when you are married. It's always better for your relationship to go out with people who have more in common with you. You are less likely to get yourself in trouble—girl or guy. Again, I am not saying never go out with your single friends, because both Joe and I do, from time to time. But, too many "Boys' Nights" at the bars or "Girls' Nights" with the single ladies can only lead to temptation.

YOU ARE NOT THAT COUPLE AT THE BAR

All that glitters isn't gold. One thing that is a big "no" is comparing yourself to your friends' and other couples' marriages.

Some guys change diapers, some guys don't. Every relationship is different. Every dynamic is different. If you're having a conversation with your girlfriend and she brags about how her husband just did three loads of laundry, folded them, and put them away, don't stomp home to your husband and bark at him for not doing it. There may be things that your husband does that your girlfriend's husband doesn't.

Marriage is not a competition. It's not a direct tit-for-tat comparison to your friend's relationship. Although Joe's underwear may never make it to the laundry basket, I have chosen to accept that flaw. He does a million things I appreciate and love. The key is figuring out what flaws you can live with and what flaws you can't. Not every drawer in the dresser is going to be closed. The milk might not get capped or replaced in the fridge. Figure out for yourself which drawers you need to be closed by your husband and close the rest yourself.

If you're envying other couples, then you're not looking for solutions to your own problems. It is wise, however, to observe the behavior of other couples to better define what you want in your own relationship. There is always room for improvement. If you see what you like in someone else's relationship, and it is something you can change yourself, then clean up your own side of the street. Like I have said throughout this book, if you change your own behavior, nine times out of ten, you will see results on the other side.

FLIRT WITH YOUR HUSBAND

Flirting openly with another man in full view of my husband? Not on your life. We're all about flirting with each other. I know some women like to get the ego boost of flirting at a party, and bring the good vibes home to their husband. Fine for them. But, I don't want or need another man's approval. I only care about Joe's. If Joe flirted with another woman in front of me, I'd slice him in half. I don't want him to look at anyone else but me in a sexy way. Intentionally making someone jealous always backfires. Instead of using your energy to try to make your husband jealous, use that energy to flirt with him. Making him feel hot and sexy will make you feel the same way.

Back in our early years, we'd go to the bar, and I'd make the rounds and talk to everyone. When we got home, Joe would say, "I feel like we didn't hang out. Like you talked to everyone else more." Now, you might think, "Why is he so needy?" He's not. Joe doesn't need me to hold his hand at a party. It's about respect and loyalty. Like the song goes, "A lady doesn't leave her escort. It isn't fair, and it's not nice. A lady doesn't wander all over the room, blowing on some other guy's dice." We arrive together. We stay near each other. We leave together. I still talk to everyone there. Plus, I shared the night with my husband. Added bonus: When we rehash what went down later on, it's easier to compare notes.

If a woman wants more attention from her husband, why turn the spotlight on another man? Let your man know that he looks good. Give him a compliment. It will be the best thing you say all night. Make eyes with your husband. Stroke his arm. Listen to his stories with the same interest you did when you were dating. He'll be grateful and flattered, and you'll feel the love reflected back at you.

TOP 3 THINGS TO NEVER SAY TO YOUR HUSBAND WHEN YOU'RE OUT ON THE TOWN

1. "WHY DON'T YOU DO LAUNDRY LIKE [FILL IN THE BLANK]?"

Never compare your husband to another man, especially when you are out on the town and having a couple drinks. Even if it is as simple as, "Hey, so and so changes diapers, why don't you?" I promise you that your husband does not want to be compared to the guy next to him. Joe hates it. This is a big no-no. Men take this as a huge insult. Add alcohol to the mix, and you will have a major blow-out fight to cap off the evening.

> If you listen to nothing else Melissa tells you, please listen to this rule #1. I can't tell you how insulting it is when we try to be your everything, and you compare us to another man. It's a big slap in the face. Listen, some men change diapers, some go food shopping, some even fold the laundry, and others work a twelve-hour day. You can't have it all. You married your husband for a reason. Try to remember what it was.

2. "YOU WANT TO LEAVE? GO AHEAD. I'LL SEE YOU AT HOME LATER."

If you go out together, you go home together. If I ever dismissed Joe like that, he'd fall over dead from shock. I might as well say, "Don't let the door hit you on the way out!" The idea of sending Joe home by himself while I stay behind partying without him? It's unthinkable. He'd never allow it, and I wouldn't want him to. It's just not in his DNA to leave a woman behind. He has a strong protector gene. What would I stay at the party for anyway? It's like my Mother always used to say to my sisters and me, "Nothing good can happen after 1:00 A.M."

My friends once suggested a girls' weekend in the Caribbean. I said, "A *weekend*??? Away from Joe and the kids? Are you crazy?" Of course, she looked at me like I was crazy. Maybe I am. Other couples socialize apart, and that's fine for them. But Joe and I stick together like glue. I know it's odd that we're always together. It's not the norm. Some may call us co-dependent or addicted to each other or just plain clingy, but, we are both fine with it. I'm not saying that my way is right or wrong, but we genuinely enjoy each other's company. Joe really is my best friend. When I'm with him, I don't feel any pressure to entertain like I'm "on display."

3. "IS THAT WOMAN PRETTIER THAN ME?"

Waste of breath, and wrong on so many levels. Asking this question screams, "I'm insecure and fishing for compliments," which actually makes the asker a lot less attractive. Confidence is sexy. Insecurity is prematurely aging. Forcing your husband to compare you to another woman is like tip-toeing into a minefield. It's entirely possible that he *does* think she's prettier than you. But he'll say, "Of course not! You're much prettier." Even the most jaded people don't like to be arm-twisted into a lie. The tiniest resentment is planted. Also, why in the world would a woman intentionally draw her husband's attention away from her and towards another woman? No! When you go out with you husband, you want his eyes on you. You want his ears on you. God knows, you want his lips on you. His hand should be on your thigh under the table. He's smelling your perfume and playing with your hair. That's seduction. Never, ever, ever intentionally direct his attention away from you. If it does go elsewhere, gently draw it back by asking a much better question, like, "Do you have any idea what I'm going to do to you later?"

THE COUPLE THAT PRAYS TOGETHER, STAYS TOGETHER

Devotion is one of my favorite words. I'm devout in a spiritual sense. And, there is no denying that I thank Jesus for everything in my life. I apply the same faith and devotion to every aspect of my life—especially my relationships. If you asked Joe to describe me in one word, it'd be "loyal." That is who I am, and who I will forever aspire to be. When a friend is disloyal to me, it's an unforgiveable betrayal. When a friend turns her

I wear my heart on my chest.

back on me—a few have in recent years; the price of fame, such as it is—I flip the off switch on them. It's as if they don't exist. Poof. Be gone. But, at the same token, my *true* friends will tell you that I am the most loyal woman alive especially when it comes to family, friends, and anyone that I love. You have to hurt me first for me to turn my back on you. And, even then, I have always been very forgiving. I think that has to do with my faith.

My deepest devotion is for my most important relationship. I'm devoted to my husband. In church, my priest once talked about the three Cs of marriage: commitment to each other and Christ, companionship, and communication. (I guess that's four Cs if you count "Christ," and who doesn't?) One way to wrap up all that sentiment into a single package is to spend time together, talking and doing fun things. Sunday morning reaffirms my devotion in God. Saturday nights are like church for marriage. We reaffirm our devotion to each other.

Now, according to the priest, it also boosts the connection when you share your passions with each other. "If one person in the couple doesn't go to church, it's not enough. If one of you is passionate about something, then the other should be willing to join you so you can be a passionate together," he says.

Joe doesn't feel he needs to go to church as much as I do. He always tells me to pray for him when I'm there. He says he talks to God every day and doesn't need to be in a particular building to do it. I still work on him all the time to get him to come with me more often. But, the net/net is that Joe and I share the same foundation when it comes to our devotion to God.

In the meantime, we're open to sharing each other's passions. Joe built me a recording studio in our basement so I could pursue my passion for singing, and he's been with me every step and song along the way. I have become a football wife, and spend half of my Sunday on the couch with Joe, cheering for the Giants. We're expanding our worlds and moving closer together at the same time.

As a couple, you can change and grow together, or you will change and grow apart.

My mother taught me how to be loyal, and also how hard it can be. Joe hasn't come close to testing my devotion the way my father tested hers. I have no idea what he'd do at this point to push me to the limit of my faith in us. Unless he cheats on me, I'm never going anywhere.

CHAPTER SIX

On TV!

I still can't quite believe that Joe and I are on a TV show. The entire ride has been unexpected and intense to say the least. To make sense of it, I think of the show as another kind of parlor, just another public place that Joe and I move around in. It's like going out to a restaurant that seats five million people. Our table is in the middle of the room, and it's as if we are talking into a loud speaker for the world to hear.

A bit odd. A little disconcerting. But, on the other hand, it seems natural to have a camera on me 24/7, too. When I was a little girl, my father used to videotape me constantly. Video cameras were a brand new thing in 1985. My father got one of the very first Sony Camcorders to hit the market. It was a heavy black box with a microphone attachment that was laughably bulky and awkward compared to the playing-card size iPhones and Flip cameras today. The Camcorder had to weight at least seven pounds. He had to rest it on his shoulder between takes.

When the original Camcorders came out, everyone rushed to get one even though they were kind of expensive. Suddenly, at school concerts and games, half the parents were lugging around their video cameras to record each precious moment. My father was no exception. But he didn't turn the thing off when the concert or game was over. He kept it rolling. The novelty didn't wear off for him. In another reality, my father might've been a director or a cinematographer. But in his short life, he was happy to videotape our family, especially me. He always called me his little star.

And, somehow my father always managed to capture every moment—the big and the small. Despite his occasional disappearances, he never missed a single school play, any of my solo singing performances, or a single game that I cheered at. I still have every VHS tape he ever made. Believe it or not, to this day, I have two VHS players in our home, just for these tapes. And, trust me, I play them all the time for Joe and the kids. They love to watch them. The best part is hearing my father's voice in the background. "Come on, Meliss! Come on!" Then, ever so slowly and softly, he would always say, "A star is born!"

I could play those tapes over and over. I never tire of hearing his voice. Those VHS tapes are like gold to me. Thank you, Daddy for making me all of those memories. Now, I film my own kids all the time, to give them the same gift.

From the age of six, he pointed and trained the lens at me. When I hammed it up, he'd crack a smile. His mouth was all I could see of his face with the black box against his eye. Seeing that flash of white and his mustache float up gave me the best feeling in the world. That smile was because of me. I made him happy. I wanted nothing more than to make that happen again and again.

In hindsight, I have to wonder if putting the Camcorder between us made it easier for us to communicate. Let's face it, most middle-age men don't really know what to say to their six-year-old daughter. And remember, he was out of practice. I was born ten years after my closest sister. Thanks to the Camcorder, my father and I didn't have to rely on words. We didn't have to play catch or kick the ball around the yard. I could sing and dance, which I adored, and he'd film me, which he loved. I'm sure it wasn't that my routines and songs were so mesmerizing. My father, like most men, cherished his electronic toys. I gave him a good reason to use it. Unlike my mother and sisters who shied away from the camera, I was always rushing in front of it. I'd jump up on the coffee table and say, "Video me! Video me!" He'd oblige and film my every move.

If there is ever a "Behind the Music" or E! True Hollywood Story about me, I will have more childhood video footage to offer producers than any other celeb in history. I have stacks of videos. Hundreds of hours of footage. The camera became this constant presence in our house. I got so used to it that when that red record light wasn't in front of me, I felt like something was missing.

I'm positive that my childhood history as the star of our family home movies was why it was relatively easy for me to accept being followed around by a camera crew for RHONJ. When a camera turns on, I fondly think of the fun my father and I had together. Call it pathological, or call it lucky. I can tell you that if you aren't happy with someone filming you from every angle, catching humiliating moments and verbal flubs, recording you at your best, not-so-best, and every moment in between, then you will die a thousand deaths on a reality show. For a lot of people, when a camera goes on they become self-conscious. Not me. I made the decision to put myself on national TV, and I told myself that if I was going to do it, I was going to be real. Some things haven't changed. For me, being in front of the camera is fun. Okay, so there is a little drama, too, but mostly it's just fun.

Ninety percent of reality success is not freezing or freaking when the camera goes on. Reality TV stardom strikes like lightning when you're exactly who you are whether the camera is on or off. It's goes beyond being comfortable in front of the camera (although that helps). It's accepting what the camera reveals about you. Because it will. You can try to present yourself as one thing. But your true nature will eventually come out. That's why the shows film round the clock, to catch that telling moment when you let your guard down.

The two biggest misconceptions about people who choose to appear on a reality show: (1) They have no shame, and (2) they're fame whores. Some reality stars do crave fame like a starving man craves a cheeseburger. Some use it as a platform to push their other projects. And, some are doing it just because, and will let it take its course. Either way, let's call a spade a spade, you don't join a reality show because you want to hide in a closet. Come on, we all know what we are getting ourselves into. It's no secret that the exposure has ruined many marriages and destroyed reputations. I've read about the *Real Housewives* Divorce Curse. If you are going to get into this, your marriage better be strong. You better make a pact that you will never let anything break your bond. Trust me. There are always haters. I always say, they are going to find where you shine the most and attack. Misery loves company. But, Joe and I refuse to engage. Instead, we embrace our haters. We've learned to love them. You're nothing without them. So, given the history, it might seem crazy to willingly test your sanity, grit, and marriage just for the possibility that maybe, if you're lucky, you'll get a jewelry line, some sort of beverage endorsement or even a music career!

So, why did Joe and I sign on? Why put ourselves under the microscope? Why risk the drama? The original appeal was to show the world how hard Joe and I work to live this life, what we've accomplished, and how we raise our kids. I'm so proud of our family, home, and our marriage. I think it's where we shine. I wanted to be able to say, "Look what we did!" It sounds corny, but I wanted to demonstrate the happiness of being a stay-at-home Mom and wifey, and to be inspiring for the women who were in my situation. It's a natural impulse, to want to show off your family, adventures, the food we cook, where we go, what we wear. Otherwise, Facebook, Twitter, and Instagram wouldn't be so popular. Well, being on RHONJ is like posting your travel and kids' birthday photos on Facebook not only for your friends, but for millions of viewers. It's Instagram on steroids.

For the record, Joe and I never called a producer. They found us. If it had been the other way around, we probably wouldn't be on the show. If we'd shown any interest, we would have been ignored. Bravo's style is, the more you want to be on the show, the less likely you are to get on it. Like a house cat, if you grab at him, he'll run under the bed. But if you sit and wait for him to come to you, he'll jump right in your lap.

I swear, if I ever get a cat, I'll name him Bravo. Although I'm deathly allergic to cats, so that may be a problem!

Before we started filming—even before we were officially cast—I had terrible anxiety about how it would affect my family. I used to toss and turn at night, imagining the best- and the worst-case scenarios.

The best case, obviously, was that I'd be popular with viewers. I'd get busy traveling, singing, and building a following for my music. There was a great scene in season 3 when I talked about my childhood fantasies of singing stardom, and the producers turned it into a funny montage with twinkling stars in my eyes. It's all true. I dreamed of being a singer when I was a little girl. That dream took a long break after my father died. But it came roaring back, thanks to Joe's encouragement.

The worst case? That the show would destroy my marriage.

I know that the show is called *The Real Housewives*, not *The Real Husbands*, but the men play a part. I knew in my heart that Joe and I had a rock-solid marriage, but I had never been on TV before, so it was the unknown. I didn't have a crystal ball, and the last thing I would ever roll the dice on is my marriage. But, after many long talks with Joe, we both decided that there was nothing that could break us, and it would be an experience and adventure for us. The best part—we could always get off the ride if we wanted to.

The other worry I had was not being able to keep up with my role as Mom and wife as Joe knew it. I vividly remember confiding in Caroline Manzo about my fears. She told me, "You're right to be afraid. You're going to get really busy in a heartbeat. Traveling, going from place to place to promote the show. But you're always wife and mother first." I really took Caroline's words to heart, and I was worried about juggling filming and what I knew had to come first in my home—my husband and my kids. Caroline's kids were older. Mine were babies. How could I do it?

I had a good life. Why risk it?

When in doubt, I prayed. I turned to God to point me in the right direction and left it in His hands. I asked God to bless us with the opportunity, but if the show started to do anything to hurt our marriage, to take it away. I'd made the same prayer countless times before. Whatever life had in store for me, if it affected my marriage in a negative way, I didn't want it.

I'm a simple guy. I go to work every day. We were married six years before we got on the show. I have a wife that doesn't leave my side. We love to be together. She's my best friend. Every night, I come home. She's in the kitchen looking cute, in those tight pants I love, cooking my favorite food. It was my dream life. I was used to that.

And then it started to change. I'm not going to lie. It took some time to get used to. I remember one time when Melissa told me that she would be out doing press for the show. When I came home, walked into the kitchen, and saw the babysitter holding little Joey, I felt a pit in my stomach. I knew who she was—I'd hired her—but I wasn't ready for the reality of not seeing my wife when I walked in the door. In that half second between what I was expecting and what I was actually seeing, I got a little nervous of what was to come.

When Melissa got home, I told her that I was bummed out. I didn't want to make her feel bad, but it was all starting to hit me. She apologized, but there was nothing to be sorry for. She did nothing wrong.

Some husbands are featured on the show more than others. I knew from the beginning, if I was going to be on the show, Joe was, too. I'm not a wife without a husband. We're a team. If I'm going to let the world into my life, Joe is a huge part of that.

My praying gave me enough courage to move forward, despite being clueless about how it would all work. *The Real Housewives of New Jersey* was a speeding train, and it threw passengers out the windows, and could go off the rails at any time. I took a deep breath and got on. I decided that the only way this would work would be to have Joe at my side like glue. We would do the show like we did everything else—together, sharing the ups and downs, every step of the way.

The first couple times I saw Melissa interviewed on TV, I was blown away. I knew she would be good at it, but she was great. She was so confident and so well-spoken. At that moment I knew that being on TV was where Melissa needed to be. I knew that she was never going to embarrass me or our family. Exactly the opposite. I was so proud of her. *I am* so proud of her. Now, the whole world gets to see what I see every day. A beautiful, strong woman, who can do it all—great mom, great wife, and still holding her own in front of millions.

It was a bumpy start. I came onto a hit show that was already established for two seasons. I was the new girl. Like moving to Boca, the girls didn't like me at first. I had to win them over. Plus, I had never been in the spotlight like this before, and even though I felt comfortable, it took time to get used to being in the public eye. I didn't expect everyone to like me. I know you can't please everyone. But, it stings when people say mean and untrue things about you. After a while, your skin gets thicker, and you learn to brush it off. You really need to have a strong sense of self. It happens so fast. And I don't think you can ever prepare yourself for sudden fame. The only way to deal with it is to stay true to who you are. It's where you go back to in any stressful situation.

My marriage philosophy of sticking side by side with Joe, and constant two-way communication, appealed to the fans. Since I wouldn't have been on the show any other way, I was glad that it worked out for us. After two seasons, fans expect to see Joe as much as they do me, and I love it. At my performances, Joe often introduces me. He's always in the front row, clapping and screaming and cheering me on. In reality and on "reality," Joe and I shine as a couple. I might have some good moments on my own, but our best moments on and off camera are as a pair. When we're recognized by fans, they yell, "It's Melissa and Joe Gorga!" Not "It's Melissa!" When they ask to take a photo, they want to stand between us.

Sharing this experience with Joe doubles the fun and halves the pain.

Reality TV holds up a mirror to reveal who you truly are. The reflection might be pretty, ugly, or both, depending on the season and situation. Joe is at my side in my reality TV mirror. We reflect each other's best intentions, flaws, positive and negative tendencies. It's not always flattering! But we are in it together. We're a team.

When you get married, you also marry your husband's family. With a big Italian family, there are a lot of big personalities, to say the least. The way I managed some of the big personalities in our family is to keep my side of the street clean. I know who I am. I have a strong set of core values. Family comes first. Period. Joe and I try to teach this to our kids by example. No matter what comes at you, you have to remember that you can only control your own actions and to take the high road.

Believe me, there have been times where Joe has lost his cool over things our family might've done. I know his passion is rooted in his strong belief that we are a team. He wants to protect me, and for that, I love him even more. Joe and I keep each other in check. At the end of each day, when we lay our heads on our pillows, we know in our hearts that we did the best that we could to handle any family issues with dignity and grace.

And, as I always like to say, "Thank you, Jesus!" I am a firm believer that what you put out into the world comes back to you tenfold. God has been good to us. We really feel so lucky and blessed.

BEST FRIENDS LAST FOREVER?

Well, not always.

I feel very strongly about the people that I'm close with. I've had most of my best girlfriends since second grade. From dolls, daydreaming, and pigtails to husbands, babies, and blowouts, we've seen it all together. I still talk to the same girls that I rode my pink and gray Huffy bike with. Maybe it's because I'm an Aries, but I don't like change much—especially with my friendships and the people I love and am close to. I'm as loyal as the day is long, and I would do anything for friends and family. And I feel certain they would do anything for me.

I never dreamed that being on TV would change that. I don't understand why some people have a hard time dealing with other people's success. I actually just read a quote that says it best, from Henry David Thoreau: "Friends . . . they cherish one another's hopes. They are kind to one another's dreams."

Before RHONJ, I had always heard that fame changed people. I've had a little taste of it. Now I think that when your life changes for the better, you don't necessarily change. But sometimes, the people around you do. I'm the same person. And, in many ways, the spotlight has actually made me more humble and vulnerable. I still pinch myself when a fan asks to take a picture with me. I really can't believe it.

I am someone who always forgives, and, as hard as it is to let a person go, you sometimes have to say goodbye to get rid of the negativity in your life. There is nothing worse than being betrayed. We've all been there. It's incredibly painful to see people you love and trust trying to sabotage your success. I've learned that is the reality of "reality."

So, ladies, as with every experience in my life, good or bad, I try to see the lesson that God is trying to teach me. With love and friendship, always take the high road and hold your head high, even when it hurts—especially when it hurts. Always remind yourself that you cannot control someone else's actions, only your own. So, take a deep breath and breathe. Being on the RHONJ, and now living my life in the public eye, has shown me that as we grow, we don't lose friends; we just learn who our real friends are.

MELISSA AND JOE PLUS THREE

The kids are so little, they don't know what's going on. Gino is just starting to ask, "Why do those people want to take your picture?" I tell him that we're on a TV show. He says, "Oh, yeah." It's all he knows! Joey was a baby when we started, so cameras and crews are all he's experienced. Antonia loves it. Her home and school life is stable and unaffected by the show. No one—even on Twitter, which can often be a seething snake pit of negativity—has anything bad to say about my children. I pray that never happens, and if it does, I'll do whatever needs to be done to keep them unaffected.

Being recognized does freak me out when I'm with the kids, though. I'm at a mall, and people stop me. I'm thinking, *I can't pose right now. I have my two-year-old with me and I can't look away from him.* They want to tell me all their stories, have me sign a million different things, take a pic, and somehow I do it all without taking my eyes off my kids. A few times, fans have pulled right up to my front door when the kids were riding their bikes out by the driveway. That makes me nervous. What do we all tell our kids from birth? Don't get in a car with anyone you don't know, even if they know your name. The fans are *yelling* their names. "Hey, Joey! Hey, Gino!" It's confusing for them that so many strangers address them like family. Several times, fans have rung my doorbell. It's usually high school girls. I'm never rude, but it's invasive. I'm usually a mess with my hair up in bun. But, I'm a people pleaser. It's so hard for me to say no. I'm still working on that.

People often ask me, "Who watches the kids when you do appearances and film?" It might seem like we're constantly filming and doing appearances. But the truth is, the show films for five months. There might be up to a year between seasons. I don't film every day, and never for an entire day. I always try to schedule any press appearances for the show during the school day, so I can get back home in time to pick the kids up, or as close to dinnertime as possible. If I can't get home in time, we use our regular babysitter. Sometimes, Joe stays home with the kids by himself. Yes! It's true! It's just another way we've evolved as a family. My performances are usually on Saturday nights. When we have to do an overnight, the kids often come along, or my sisters and mother watch them. My kids are blessed with the best *zias* (aunt in Italian) and and *nonnas* (Grandmas) in the world! And, it makes me feel good knowing that if Joe and I are away, that my kids are with family. It's a win-win. My kids get to enjoy special time with their Nonni, and Joe and I enjoy special time with each other.

The one thing I'm sure of is that when my time in the spotlight is over, my family will still be here. So, as I'm enjoying the ride, my husband and kids will always come first. I'd give up anything for them. I'll always do everything in my power to make them happy.

TELEVISION ON THE TOILET

. . . .

Joe and I have both had the rotten experience of a best friend turning their backs on us when we got on the show. All of the sudden, they started to make impossible demands on us and expect things from us we couldn't deliver. The sad truth is that it was usually about money. "Film at my store!" "Plug in my business!" "Bring me on RHONJ so I can sell my whatever!" As cast members, we don't always have a say over where we film.

I had a friend who gave photos of us doing crazy teenage stuff together in a media outlet. The photo was of me, peeing on a toilet. Something I do five times a day. Something we all do five times a day. She dug out these fifteen-year-old snapshots? Really! Does it get any more ordinary and boring than that?

Now, if I were taking a poopie, I'd understand. Wow. Much more interesting. Stop the presses. Joe probably would have bought that photo himself, just to have proof that I actually poop! I never let him see me do it. Because I just don't. We all know girls don't poop!

At the end of my first season on RHONJ, *US Weekly* magazine wanted to put me in their "Hot Bodies 2012" issue. They said it would possibly be a cover. Wow! A *positive* cover. Yes, please! They offered to fly me to California for the day, put me up in a hotel, and send me home the next day.

I was thrilled and beyond flattered. I immediately called Joe. I learned later on that magazines never promise the cover. Depending on what goes on in the world, the cover photo could change at the last minute. Never believe it until you see it.

Joe said, "No. You can't just fly around whenever you want." The longer we talked, the harder his line. This was around the same time my first single, "On Display," hit the iTunes charts. For six years, I had been the dutiful wife with my whole world centered around my family and home. And now it was only six months into being on RHONJ, and I was starting to get requests that would take me away from family and home. I had to pause. *How was I going to "do it all?"* In an instant, I thought, *Maybe you can't have it all, the happy marriage, family, and career.* But I wanted it all. I had to figure it out a way to make it work.

What's interesting is that Joe's objection had nothing to do with the fact that I was going to pose in a bikini for a magazine. After many honest and sometimes hard conversations later, I figured it out. Joe was worried. He was worried that if I was flying to L.A. to do a photo shoot on a Wednesday, then what was going to be on my schedule for a Thursday? How far would this go? How much bigger would it get?

I didn't blame him. I was having a lot of the same feelings. We had a really good life. My dream life, in fact. Why fix what isn't broken? I couldn't deny that flying cross-country with only a week's notice to do a photo shoot in a bikini was pretty far from "old-school Italian values." But, I wasn't trying to deny that. I was trying to find a way to mesh my two worlds. I loved being a good wife and mother and did not want that part of my world to change in any way. I just wanted to sprinkle in some RHONJ fun, and the opportunity to explore focusing on my music. As soon as I realized that Joe and I shared the same fears and were on the same page, we started trying to figure out how we could do it all together. Side note: This is the perfect example of what I think happens in many marriages. Often, the biggest fights are rooted in miscommunication. If you take a breath, slow down, and really try to listen to your partner, you may really hear what he is trying to say. And, when you hear his truth, you may even find your own.

That first trip to L.A. set the tone for how Joe and I work together in order to balance RHONJ and our family life. We decided we would use that overnight trip as a romantic getaway. We spent the day at the pool when I wasn't shooting. Went to a great dinner. Spent the night in a great hotel. Then home the next day. My mother watched the kids. I was thrilled. Joe was thrilled. My kids were thrilled. I remember when our flight landed at Newark after an amazing twenty-four-hour mini-cation. I thought to myself, *I think this is going to be okay.* Thank you, Jesus!

That photo shoot remains my favorite to this day. I think it's Joe's, too. What could have been a wedge between us turned into memories we'll cherish for the rest of our lives. When we're old and gray, I'll be thanking God I have proof that my body once looked that sexy! The fight over the shoot was an ice breaker. Joe and I both understand now that no matter what opportunities come my or our way, we're not going anywhere—in a figurative and literal sense—without each other. (Ladies, ladies, as corny as this all sounds, it works! The more you love together and hang together, the stronger your marriage will be.)

We all know the high stakes of going on a reality show. For us, it's become even more complicated with family. That's been difficult. It felt like people were trying to destroy us. Fans took sides in an extreme way. In the beginning, the pressure really got to Melissa. That killed me. I didn't want to come home and find my wife stressed. For what? Because a stranger insulted her on Twitter? Who cares?

It's been three years, and we've learned how to live this way. Now, the logistics of filming are nothing. We make adjustments. We used to live a good life—simple and extravagant in our own way. Then it changed. People are in your home all the time. My wife has to be in a different state. We have to roll with things and tweak old routines.

It changes you. Are you going to argue and have meltdowns? Sometimes, yes. But we've learned not to let people on blogs get to us. They write that I'm cheating, doing drugs, all kinds of nonsense. In the beginning, we didn't know how to handle the lies and the stress. Now we know.

How to deal with it? Simple. Ignore it. It's white noise in the background. The article might of had our names in it, but it has nothing to do with who we are as individuals or as a family. We know who we are. We know what we do, and what we've done. Any magazine or person that puts out a lie about us doesn't change who we really are. We have a strong sense of self. If you don't, any pressure from the outside can wreck you.

Now, not every couple will have fights about how to handle overnight pseudo-celebrity and viscous lies published about their marriage. But every couple deals with challenges and shifts in the dynamic of the relationship that might make one or the other feel insecure. Women underestimate that men can be needy and insecure, too. Men put on a strong front. I would say that ninety percent of the conflicts in my marriage stem from someone's feeling getting hurt. When Joe feels defensive, he goes on the offensive. Me, too. We're very similar in that way.

Deal with the doubt, and trust falls right back into place. Now Joe is raring to go on little overnights. I think he looks forward to my concerts in Atlantic City and the Poconos more than I do.

I wouldn't be a "star," whatever that means, if it weren't for the inspiration and affirmation I get from my marriage. My most popular song on iTunes—"How Many Times"—was written for and about Joe. It rose all the way up to number four on the charts. The reason it was such a hit? Fans had an emotional reaction to a song about my love for Joe. When I thought about writing a book, the first thing that came to mind was to talk about marriage, how ours works, why ours works, and ideas to inspire other women to improve theirs. "How are you guys so in love and make your marriage work? Is it really true?" is the number one question I get asked by fans on Facebook, Twitter, and in-person at events.

Joe and I have grown even closer by being on the show. Sure, we've had our fights about how to figure out schedules, etc. But when we needed support and encouragement, we have turned towards each other for it. Going through it side by side has been a constant reminder that the show hasn't changed us. We are fundamentally the same—only stronger.

People can come up to us at a restaurant, and Melissa treats them all with respect. Every time I see her sweet way, I know she's the same person. Seeing and knowing that she's the same girl I fell in love with makes me love her even more. I never thought it was possible to love her more. But I do. Every day.

My RHONJ story line is a love story. Whatever I might do season to season, the A-plot is our marriage. It's also the B-plot and the C-plot. The greatest blessing of being on the show is watching our marriage—seeing the love between us. I was afraid that joining the cast would harm my marriage. But after three years, it's done the opposite. We're hotter and stronger than ever.

STAGE FRIGHT

I'm completely at ease in front of any camera. I can sing into a hairbrush in the mirror with the best of them. But, get on stage, in front of a crowd of real life people? Scary.

Even if you hire a top choreographer to teach you (shout out, Cris Judd!), you're only as good as your ability and determination. No matter how many backup dancers and musicians are on stage behind you, when you're upfront, the center of attention, you are alone. Eyes on you. Expectations on you. It can be a lonely place—or the greatest spot in the world. You have only

Fierce! At Splash in NYC last year.

yourself, the hours of sweat you've put into a performance, and your raw courage to get you through. One thing I learned from Cris—and this applies to singing on stage, presenting a Power-Point at work, any public speaking or performance on any level—is to command attention with stillness. Just stand still. Make the audience look at you, and listen to you. If you can stand still and capture their attention, you've got them in the palm of you hand. I had to learn that the hard way. I fought the urge to move around. When I found my own still center, it was like discovering gravity.

That didn't come right away. It took a while. Now I perform with minor stage fright and maximum energy for thousands—it's like an adrenaline rush. As soon as a song is over, you don't want to get off the stage. You want more and more. The energy from the crowd amps me up every single time. It boggles my mind. If I do quake in my boots, I have another trick to calm myself down. When everyone is looking at me, I look down to the edge of the stage and find Joe in the front row cheering me on. You know that old saying, "To get over stage fright, picture the audience in their underwear?" Well, I just picture Joe Gorga. I will leave the rest of the details to you. Needless to say, it puts a bounce in my step and smile on my face.

In our modern-yet-old-fashioned marriage, we have each other's back. It's not traditional to sing in a sequin bodysuit at Splash nightclub in NYC, but I have! And Joe got the party started by introducing me to the crowd. He gushed! He's my number one fan, and I'm his. As long as you know you've got the most important person in your life rooting for you, you can do just about anything, and face down any fear. I hope anyone who's watching thinks so, too. Joe and I are both so humbled by this whole experience. When I say, "Thank you, Jesus," I really mean it!

CHAPTER SEVEN

Staying In

A lot of my friends go to a strip club every night after work. I'm not that guy. Who needs to stare at strippers when my sexy wife is waiting for me at home?

That's my man. That's why I married him. But I'm going take a little credit here. I make him *want* to come home. In fact, he hardly wants to leave! Joe and I are homebodies. Everything we want or need is here. Home is comfort. It's sanctuary. It's also a meeting place for our friends and family. We're not only hunkering down with each other, we have an open-door policy. The "parlor" is the living room, the kitchen, the den, the backyard—all the common spaces in our home where we entertain guests and hang out as a family.

ENTERTAINING ITALIAN STYLE

Italians are a social people. We surround ourselves with family, music, conversation. We talk over each other, get up in each other's business. Put an Italian in solitary confinement, and she'll claw at the walls after ten minutes. It might seem that we throw so many parties on RHONJ so we can film together. But the truth is, we need loud parties like some people need quiet time. I could write a whole book about throwing parties (and I just might!). In this book about marriage, though, I want to talk about how bringing other people into our sanctuary keeps our union strong.

Make your husband feel happy and entertained at home, and he won't look to go elsewhere.

WORK HARD TO PLAY HARD

Okay, ladies, I know it's a lot of work to have people over. You have to cook, entertain, and clean up, but it's all worth it. Parties keep your house alive. What's more homey than a kitchen full of women in aprons, shoulder to shoulder, chopping vegetables and stirring pots, with mouthwatering smells pouring from the ovens? What says happy family more than a backyard full of kids running around, laughing; fathers watching them from the deck, bottles of beer in their hands, trash talking each other? I love it. Filling my house with people, delicious smells and laughter was my childhood fantasy of the perfect adulthood. Few things give me the same sense of accomplishment than throwing a big party, feeding dozens of people, and making them so comfortable and content that they don't want to leave.

Some of our parties are elaborate affairs that take weeks of planning, like the Thanksgiving dinner shown on RHONJ. We had thirty people over and set up a banquet table in our front hallway. We used nearly every piece of china, silverware, and crystal we have to serve the feast, including a 30-pound turkey. That bird barely fit in the oven. It took seven hours to roast it! I'd never worked so hard in my life to create that meal. But I got to see everyone I care about drooling over it, and savoring every bite. That's my bliss.

Some of our parties are impromptu spur-of-the-moment casual gatherings. One couple stops by for lunch, and we call in another and another. Before you know it, we've got four families in the backyard, and they're hungry. That's my favorite kind of meal, when you have to be spontaneous in the kitchen. A test of my cooking skills gets my creative juices flowing. I pretend that I'm on an episode of *Top Chef.*

When Joe sees me running around, making sure everyone is taken care of, he bursts with pride. With one exception (guess), he never loves me more that when I'm making pasta and meatballs for our friends and family. So what if the kitchen and floors get dirty? We don't live in a museum. It's a *home*, bursting with life, kids running around, food everywhere, drinks, laughter, and love.

Entertaining is great for all of us. Joe hangs with his buddies and shows off the house he built and the beautiful yard. The kids get all-day playdates with their crew. I spend the day with my girls.

HUNGRY?

Doesn't matter if it's a backyard barbecue, a pool party, a formal dinner, or an informal brunch, I put out a massive spread of food. The table must sag under the weight of all the platters and dishes upon it. Just as you can always take one more step, you can always fix one more dish.

THIRSTY?

The wine must flow like a river. When I walk through the house during a party, I make sure every hand has a glass in it. Alcohol always lifts the party mood. But in a hot, crowded room, people can get dehydrated, which can make you drag. Drinking ensures high energy and lower inhibitions. It's not a party if someone doesn't say or do something they regret in the morning.

KEEP THE GUESTS GUESSING

I like to throw in a few unexpected twists and turns. At our big Thanksgiving party, Joe surprised our guests with an inflatable bull-riding ring in the yard. At our pool party, we broke out cans and had a whipped cream fight. When our guests are doubled over laughing, and saying, "Only at the Gorgas!" I know we're a hit.

SPARE NO EXPENSE

The happiness of your family and friends is at stake. So buy the steak! Filling bellies and souls doesn't come cheap. It's a question of respect. You shower your guests with the best, and they know you care about them. Whatever you put out there in life or on the table—kindness, love, and quality meats—it flows right back to you.

YOU CAN'T HAVE TOO MANY COOKS IN AN ITALIAN KITCHEN

I love it when guests offer to roll meatballs and stir the sauce. Anyone who wanders into the kitchen and wants to put on an apron or pick up a spoon is welcome! It's not like I have to ask. My sisters and mother are just like me. As soon as they enter a house, they go straight to the kitchen and roll up their sleeves. With your eyes on the chopping board or the sauce, the talk can get pretty wild. Cooking together is a great way to get to know new people. When half of the brain is busy doing one thing, the other half opens up. Your guard comes down. I've had some of the most intimate, revealing conversations while cooking. It's better than alcohol for loosening the lips.

THE HOSTESS WITH THE MOSTEST

If I'm well dressed, none of my guests will feel overdressed and uncomfortable. They won't feel underdressed either, because, chances are, I'll be wearing an apron over my outfit. I do my hair and makeup. If people are making the effort to come over, it's my obligation to look decent for them, and to show I made the extra effort on their behalf. It just sets a tone of appreciation and respect, and puts guests in a festive mood. Also, I know that if Joe sees me from across the crowded room, he'll like what he sees. We play eye contact cat and mouse when we entertain at home, sneaking peeks at each other, checking each other out, sending sexy telepathic messages about what we'll do when everyone leaves. Parties are like extended foreplay for us.

THE DOWNSIDE OF ENTERTAINING

At the end of the day, my face aches from smiling so hard.

JUST DESSERTS

After everyone *finally* leaves, Joe rubs my shoulders and says, "What a woman I have." My whole body vibrates with pride. When I eventually fall asleep, it's the best feeling of satisfaction, knowing I got to please everyone, including myself.

FIVE THINGS I WILL NEVER SAY WHEN ENTERTAINING MY IN-LAWS

1. **"SERVE YOURSELF."**

   No! They didn't drive all the way over to our place to be treated like they never left home. I bend over backwards when I entertain my in-laws. It's a given. I take their coats and hang them up. I put food on their plates and bring it to them. It's about *respect*! In Italian families, the daughter-in-law has a lot to prove. Joe is a real mama's boy. When his mother and father come over for dinner, I have to show my mother-in-law that Joe is being well fed and treated with respect in his own home.

2. "I'M USING PLASTIC PLATES."

The day I give my mother-in-law a plastic plate is the day I die of mortification. When I prepare dinner for them, I use the good china. If I serve a Coke, it'll be in a crystal glass. Yes, plastic might make cleanup easier. When we have a pool party at our shore house, I use paper and plastic. But for the in-laws? Plastic is an insult! Twenty years from now, they'd say, "Remember the time Melissa gave us plastic plates?"

3. "WOW, WE ATE EVERYTHING."

I make enough food for guests to have four servings if they want. My in-laws are very traditional and the menu must have a meat course, a fish course, a cheese plate, a pasta course, and hot vegetables. Now, they might not touch a dish. But it will be there for them regardless. The worst criticism my father-in-law could make is, "She didn't give me enough to eat." So I make sure he has nothing to complain about.

4. "I'VE GOT AN EARLY MORNING."

Rushing my in-laws to leave would be another insult. They came a long way to see their grandchildren, and they're welcome to stay as long as they like. I will continue to serve them and make them comfortable until they're ready to go. And even then, I'll ask them if there's anything else I can do. Are you seeing the common theme? I am their slave from the minute they walk in until the minute they go.

5. "GLAD THAT'S OVER."

Joe would kill me if I griped about entertaining his

family or being happy to put another night with them in the books. Family is everything to both of us.

CHILLING ITALIAN STYLE

We don't entertain every weekend. Families need their downtime, too. We relish Sundays with just us, chilling in our pajamas on the couch with the kids, crawling on top of each other like little monkeys. I'll bake cookies. We watch the Giants, eat, talk, and play with the kids. Half the time, they're doing something funny and we crack up. Antonia shows us her cheers. Gino dresses up like Spider-Man with Joey as his sidekick, Batman. When it's cold, we snuggle under blankets on the couch, coming out only to go to the kitchen to get more food. We all work so hard during the week. Joe busts his ass at work. I have my career, the house, and the kids. They have homework and activities. But the weekend is our time to slow down, recharge, and count our blessings. You can cram a lot of bonding into those two days.

Our Weekend Timeline:

Friday Nights. We celebrate the end of the work/school week by taking the kids out to a child-friendly restaurant. It's fun for them to get out of the house. It's also our weekly lesson in proper manners and table etiquette. Children who misbehave at restaurants are taught that it's okay to run wild by permissive parents. Even in a family restaurant, we make sure the kids behave properly.

Saturday. Joe goes into the office or out to a building site for a couple of hours. While he does that, I get some stuff done around the house. If we're lucky and the kids have playdates, we might go to the gym in the afternoon.

Saturday Night. Date night!

Sunday Morning. Sunday is Joe's day. He's not allowed to go to the gym or to do an estimate on a building. During the week, he's up and out of the house by 6:00 A.M. On Sundays, he sleeps in. I tell him, "I want to wake up with you in my bed." We grab as much snuggling time as we can before the kids run into our room and start jumping on the bed. We wrestle with them until they start demanding breakfast. They know what's coming. Every Sunday, Joe makes pancakes. It's the one thing he knows how to cook. Oh, and eggs, too. He's been making it every Sunday for ten years, so he's perfected his recipe. After we eat, Antonia and I go to church at 9:00 for the sermon and then she has CCD (translation for non-Catholics: CCD is catechism to make communion and confirmation, aka bible study). The boys are too young, still. Soon, they'll come with me to church. One of these days, I'll convince Joe to be regular, too.

Sunday Pancakes à la Joe Gorga

INGREDIENTS:

2 cups Bisquick

1½ cups whole milk

4 eggs

olive oil

butter

chocolate chips

a banana, blueberries, strawberries, your choice of fruit

1. Combine the Bisquick, milk, and eggs in a bowl and beat until the batter is mixed.
2. Joe makes thin pancakes, like Italian crepes. If the batter isn't thin enough, add more milk, 1 tablespoon at a time.
3. Heat the olive oil in your skillet. When it smokes, pour the batter in a ¼ cup per pancake.
4. When the edges brown, flip the pancakes and brown on the opposite side.
5. When done on both sides, slide them onto a plate.
6. When still hot, plop some butter in the middle. Cut a piece out of the middle where the butter is, and eat that first.

Improvise variations with chocolate chips and diced fruit in the batter, or just put the fresh fruit on top.

Yum. Salivating for Sunday.

Sunday Afternoon. Family time. We go outside for a fun activity, weather permitting. Or we stay home, cuddle, read, watch TV, and eat all day long.

Sunday Night. Sunday dinner is a great Italian tradition. I start defrosting meat at 10:00 A.M. I'm cooking by noon. We eat in the early afternoon, around 3:00 P.M., and don't really stop. I make a huge pasta dish for late-night snacking. We're in bed by 10:00 P.M., happy and exhausted.

THE LITTLE THINGS

Joe and I do tiny things every day to make each other feel special. Small gestures make a huge impact. If you pick one or two of the items on this list, I guarantee that day-to-day tension in your marriage will gradually disappear. You'll have fewer fights. Feelings of anger and resentment will be replaced by gratitude and love. It does work both ways, so show your husband this list. He might think it's stupid. But say, "Just try it. Consider reading the list one of the little things you do for me."

FOR HER

- A kiss on his ear when he walks by. Give him a zing out of the blue.
- Surprise him with breakfast in bed. It doesn't have to be a fancy omelet and a mimosa. Just a toasted bagel and coffee shows you care.
- Buy him socks and underwear. I have no idea why men go through socks and underwear so quickly. But making sure he always has new pairs make a man feel appreciative.
- Suppress a nag. This is a small thing that you *don't* do, but he'll notice and will be so very grateful, he might just up and do the thing you would have nagged him about.
- Call his mother just to say "hello." A five-minute phone call will earn you points for a week.

FOR HIM

- Tell your wife she's beautiful twice a day. Eye contact is a must!
- Rub her shoulders while watching TV. She's had a long day, too, and the mini-massage acknowledges it.
- Compliment a specific part of her outfit. It doesn't have to be eloquent. A simple, "Nice shirt," is enough.
- Shower before bed. Extra points: Shave before bed.

PART THREE

· ·

Cook in the Kitchen

Everyone knows the expression, "the kitchen is the heart of the home." In an Italian family, the kitchen really is where all the magic happens. Our food tastes so good because we put love in it. We cook with our heart and our soul. And, Joe says that my food tastes even better when I cook it while wearing my tight black stretch pants! Hey listen, I would like to say that I was a great cook from day one, but that's not true. It took me a while to get "Gorga-approved." I had a lot to live up to, with Joe's parents coming straight from Italy, cooking the most amazing, authentic Italian food. You just can't beat that. I called my mother-in-law every single night for the first year of our marriage, asking her exactly how to make her best dishes, so I could please my man.

Ladies: Those of you who have issues with your in-laws, *don't* put my book down just yet. I know this sounds like a big pill to swallow, but I'll explain. Lucky for me, I love my mother-in-law, but I know for some of you, you must be rolling your eyes at the thought of calling yours every night. Hold tight. It pays off. Trust me. Joe was blown away. And, your husband will be, too. (I'll get into this more later.)

The action in the kitchen goes way beyond just cooking. It's conversations, loving, laughing, fighting—the works. A well-Gorganized kitchen gives me a sense of order. When the floor and counters are clean and shiny, my OCD brain can relax. Yes, I am that girl that cleans up as I cook. I sometimes even annoy myself. Why can't I just enjoy the process of cooking without keeping tidy along the way? I take pride in keeping a beautiful home and cooking delicious meals for my family. Joe is the King; I'm the Queen. The house is our castle. The kitchen is where we live and breathe.

CHAPTER EIGHT

· ·

Frystyle

At my baby shower with my mother-in-law,
nine months pregnant.

My mother cooked nearly every night. When I got home from school, she was in the kitchen. That's the old-school Italian way. She was—*is!*—a great cook, and has made that a focus in her life. Growing up, I pitched in and learned the basics. During college, I was too busy to make meals for myself. It was easier to slap together a sandwich or heat up something frozen. I didn't have serious motivation to improve my cooking skills until I got together with Joe.

No one cooks for a man like his mama, and I married a real mama's boy. When we first got married, Joe missed his mother's cooking. Anyone would. Words can't describe what incredible cooks my in-laws are. My mother-in-law and father-in-law can turn garlic, olive oil, salt, and a box of angel hair pasta into a feast that you'll never forget.

Eager to please my new husband, I watched them like a hawk as they prepared food. It didn't look all that complicated. They didn't use crazy gadgets. So when Joe asked me for dinners like his parents made for him, I said, "No problem." I was up for the challenge. I thought, *How hard can it be?* I had no idea. The Gorgas made cooking look effortless and easy, but that couldn't be further from the truth.

To learn to cook like them, I had to take lessons from them directly. I went to see my mother-in-law. I wasn't sure if she'd be willing to help me, but I had to ask. I found her in the kitchen (where else?), and said, "I want to cook for your son the way he's used to. Will you show me?" For her son, she'd do anything.

And so began my education in Italian cooking alla Gorga. I called her every night to talk me through making Joe's favorite dishes like chicken bruschetta, lentils and, especially, tagliatelle pasta with peas and ham—oh, and of course, Sunday Sauce! In addition to our phone calls, my in-laws came over once a week to cook with me. I studied them with laser focus. For a while there, Joe's mother and I barely exchanged a single word that wasn't about food and cooking. Fortunately, we could talk about that one subject for hours at a time—in particular, how I was messing it up.

I did everything wrong, from slicing tomatoes to cutting the bread to boiling water. Don't think you can screw up boiling water? Wrong. Old-school Italians are very set in their ways and speak their mind. My in-laws are no exception, and, they're usually right! They watched every turn of the knife, day after day, and always had something to say. I took some of the criticism personally, but, in hindsight, I got it. If they hadn't corrected every technique, I wouldn't have known what I was doing wrong. I was driven to impress both of them. It seemed like a test that I simply had to pass. I had to prove that I could listen and learn. Slowly, the comments tapered off. It wasn't replaced with compliments, but I was getting things right more often than wrong. They could see I was a good woman who wanted to learn and make their son happy.

Every night, apron on, I'd copy my mother-in-law's recipes and hold my breath until Joe took his first bite. "Does it taste right? Like your Mom's?" I asked, eager for feedback. Everyone knows that Joe calls it like it is and is brutally honest. He would always finish his meal, but usually had some constructive criticism. A little more salt. A little less oil. A lot more flavor.

I would always go back and try again. After a couple years, Joe couldn't tell the difference between my cooking and his Mom's. Victory! I'd set a goal, and reached it. It felt like I had cracked the Gorga cooking code, as if I'd been struggling to understand a foreign language, studying everyday but only hearing gibberish until suddenly the sounds became words and the words had meaning. I hadn't yet learned Italian. But I'd become fluent in Italian cooking.

Okay, back to those of you who would rather eat glass than

call your mother-in-law. When it comes to in-laws, whether it's cooking advice, parenting advice or any other advice, just bite your tongue. It's always hard to mesh two different families. There's your way, their way, and the right way. What I have come to realize is that the downside of fighting with your in-laws is way worse than fighting with your husband, which is what will happen if the sparks really fly. At the end of the day, you are putting your husband in the middle of a fight he will never win. Even if your husband thinks his Mom is wrong, he doesn't always want to tell her. You shouldn't either. Always remember, blood is blood. It's thicker than water. A mother is a mother is a mother. Tread lightly. If you can stay focused on making your husband happy, you won't want to tell off your mother-in-law. It just won't be worth it, because at the end of the day, the old saying always holds true: "A son is a son 'til he takes a wife, a daughter's a daughter the rest of her life." What I have learned over the years is "don't take it personally." No girl will ever be good enough for an Italian Mom's baby boy.

My in-laws are old-school Italian. They are very hard knocks. They are not going to gush over you, tell you that you're perfect or wonderful twenty-four hours a day. It's just not their way. You can tell by their little gestures, and I know in my heart, that they love the wife and mother I am, and would have never picked another woman for their son. They show their love and affection by spending time with us, sitting around the dinner table for hours. So learning how to cook with them was a huge chapter in my relationship with Joe.

I can almost hear the reaction from some of you. Really? Slave over a hot stove with your mother-in-law to please your man?

You bet I did. I wanted to make him feel like he'd get the best food of his life at home, prepared by me, the woman who took a vow to make him happy. Food is *so* important to him. (It's *so* important to every man.) He asked me to learn to cook. If I hadn't tried, it would have been like throwing his request back in his face. What he appreciated even more than my technique was the effort I put into the process.

In the end, Joe got the food he loves. I acquired an invaluable skill that, five years later continues to give me enormous satisfaction. I demonstrated my love for him by improving myself. Isn't that the clear sign of a healthy relationship? We ask and receive. We better ourselves for each other. We both reap the rewards. I never would have taken the time or been inspired to learn to cook if it weren't for Joe and the kids. Now I can do it like I was born with a wooden spoon in my hand. Joe is extremely proud of my skills. I'm even more proud of myself.

Added bonus: I got to spend a lot of time with his mother and show her how hard I was willing to work for her son's sake. As the daughter-in-law, I had a lot to prove. By her measure, if I couldn't cook well for my husband, I'd failed as a wife.

The Italian recipe for marital bliss is just that basic:

Food = love.

Cooking = respect.

If you can't cook and are unwilling to learn, you're not only being disrespectful to your husband, but to the entire Italian tradition that prizes the family meal as sacred. Cooking brings the family together, and eating seals the bond. When the food is amazing, people stay at the table longer and grow even closer. They're warmed and comforted from the inside out.

Food isn't only life sustaining. It's soul nurturing. As an eater, I can taste the care and passion that goes into a beautifully prepared meal. As a cook, I know just how much care goes into it every step along the way. There's art in being a superb chef. But to be a fabulous home cook, all it takes is determination, love, and practice, practice, practice.

COOKING ITALIAN STYLE

I consider myself an amateur cook still (twenty years from now, I'll give myself an upgrade), so I won't give specific tips and tricks about salting vegetables or softening meat. I can explain how I approach a frying pan, though. Cooking is as much attitude as it is about technique.

NO SKIMPING

Say you were preparing a meal for the President, the Pope, or Beyoncé. You'd choose only top-quality ingredients. The vegetables would be fresh. The steak would be a prime cut. You would not give a VIP frozen food or cheap meat. I happen to cook for VIPs four or five nights a week: my husband and kids. If you're going to spend extra on something, let it be food.

NO SHORTCUTS

Each drizzle of oil has meaning. Every cut takes precision. Shortcuts like chopping instead of thinly slicing means you rushed. If you don't care about the details, then you don't care about the people who will be eating your food. When I cook the right way and take my time to do it right, the love and respect shines through. The food looks and tastes better. Don't believe me? The proof is in the pasta fazool.

STRESS A MESS

I clean up while I go. Can't help myself.

GET THE KIDS TO HELP

Antonia is my sous-chef. At seven, a child is old enough to stir and chop. Prepping dinner is a great way to spend time with the kids. They like it even better than their toys. By the time Antonia is grown up and feeding her own family, cooking will be as natural to her as breathing.

SERVICE ITALIAN STYLE

Presentation—in the food and server—is everything.

DINNER IS READY WHEN JOE GETS HOME FROM WORK

Yes, I cook dinner for my husband. I serve it to him on a nice plate. I consider this my job. If I didn't do it, I'd feel like a slacker. This house rule shocks people, which shocks me. For all Joe does for this family, I can do this one thing for him. He wants a hot meal at dinnertime. He's been working all day long and comes home hungry. And I don't mind cooking it.

> To be on the same level, everyone has to get off the high horse. I don't care if the woman makes more money than the man, if he's a janitor and she's the president. After a fourteen-hour workday, if a man comes home and there's no dinner on the table, and his wife is on the phone, watching TV, or on the computer ignoring him, he won't feel respected.

CHANGE BEFORE DINNER

I know it's tempting to wear sweats all day and night. For most of the day, I do. But before Joe gets home, I change into my fold-over gym pants. They're tight and hug my curves. He sits at the table while I finish making his dinner. I giggle inside knowing that as I bend over the stove, he's definitely checking me out. I love to tease him. He knows what I'm doing, and loves it, too. Changing out of sweats is a small thing. But it can really enhance my night.

TRADE UP

I'd like to cook dinner for my family five nights a week. But since I started doing the show, it's not always possible to be home in time to fix something nice. My goal is to cook at least three nights a week, and rely on takeout for the other two. (Friday is our family restaurant night; Saturday is date night with Joe.) That said, takeout gets special treatment. Even if it's Chinese, I transfer the food from the containers to a nice plate. I get him a drink in a glass with ice. It takes two seconds, and it shows I care.

MANNERS MATTER

Just because you're married is no excuse to throw common courtesy and politeness out the window. Couples can get too comfortable, too casual. We're not formal, but Joe and I have some pretty strict rules for behavior at the table.

1. SHUT DOWN.
No phones or devices at the table. This goes for Joe and

me, and the kids. If one of the kids brought a device to the table, Joe would be *furious*. We have this rule for two reasons. For one, it's just plain rude to stare at a phone when you're eating with others. And two, it creates an emotional disconnect. I've been to restaurants with couples who e-mail and text when they're sitting next to each other at a tiny table. It's insane. How far down the rabbit hole do people have to fall before they put down the phone and communicate in real life? I don't care what carrier you have or how witty your texts, communicating electronically does your relationship a disservice. You're living parallel lives. Shut it all off and be each other's entire universe for half an hour. Look each other in the eye. Really listen to each other. It takes five minutes of undivided attention to make a genuine connection. And don't forget, your kids are watching. If they see you not talking to each other, that's what they'll do later.

2. STAY PUT.

Joe feels strongly about this one, too.

> When my father came home from work, no one was allowed to get up from the dinner table until he was done. If he sat at the table for an extra hour, we did, too. He was the King of the castle, and we respected him. I don't expect my kids to sit still for an entire hour. I can't sit still that long either. But I do insist on the same respect. They have to be excused by me before they get up.

3. SAY IT.

I personally can't imagine being so casual with my family that we don't say "please" and "thank you" when we pass the salt. When someone sneezes, we say, "God bless you." As soon as you get lax and let manners slide at home, then children—and adults—forget to say the words when they're in public. I try my hardest to make polite kids. Nothing bothers me more than bratty children.

· ·

CHAPTER NINE

Fightstyle

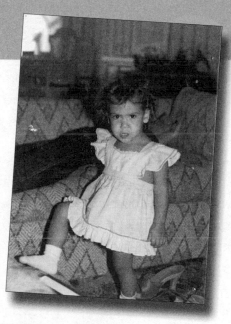

"Don't mess with me!"

No marriage is perfect. No man is perfect. Joe has his flaws, for sure. I'm not perfect either. The flaws in ourselves and in our marriage cause us to fight. When we do, it's *loud*. He's a passionate man, and I'm a passionate woman. Our fights go from 0 to 90 in about 2.5 seconds. He's a

Leo and I'm an Aries. Those epic power struggles and clashes of big egos began almost immediately after we said, "I do."

I guess you can say, Joe and I give 110 percent in everything we do. Even fighting. Fortunately, our big blowouts are rare, and we never argue in front of the kids. We've had some spectacular fights in public (see below), but usually, we unleash our anger in private.

You have to remember that even in the best marriages, fights do happen. Granted, not all couples need to scream. Some can work out all their differences without raising their voices and blood pressure. I do believe that the more passionate a marriage is in the bedroom, the more intense the fights can play out elsewhere. Our style is to express ourselves passionately, whether we're making love or making a point. The key is to remember that this, too, shall pass, and focus on getting back to a better place. Make your husband your best friend and cut him some slack.

I lose it. It's true. But I'd never let loose if I didn't believe Melissa understood me, and can handle me. It's another version of trust. I trust her to take my words and feelings at face value.

What goes unsaid can kill a marriage. If I have a complaint, it's specific. I express my unhappiness with a behavior. It's never a character assassination. I air out the grievance. She has every right to do the same thing—and Melissa takes every opportunity, believe me. I welcome it. If you have something to say, then say it! That's how I was brought up. A small problem can turn into a big one unless you fix it early. I know it might seem weird. But yelling at each other is really a sign of courtesy and respect.

MARRIAGE TORPEDOS

What goes boom in our marriage? The old saying is that a couple might fight about a thousand different things, but they're really fighting about only one. For us, ninety-nine percent of the time we fight, it's about nuances of respect. Are we making each other feel appreciated and acknowledged? If not, then we let each other know. Specifically, some of ours greatest hits were over:

FIGHTING ITSELF

A fight about fighting, aka the Meta Fight. Joe holds a grudge for a long time. He's extremely stubborn and gets himself mad just so he can stay mad. When we duke it out, I can get over it the same day. But Joe reacts the opposite way sometimes. He decides that the fight itself is a huge deal. He draws it out. For a week, he won't look at me. Now, if I felt insulted or hurt, I'd never prolong the pain for that long. I prefer to move on as soon as possible. I'm impulsive. Whatever's bothering me comes on quickly, and I get over it just as fast. I'd rather battle it out and move on. But Joe's got his pride. He can sink his teeth into an issue and not let it go. That pisses me off. I yell at him to get over it already, and then the whole thing reignites. The only defuser that makes a dent in his sulk is to ask, "Don't you love me?" Even if he's furious, he'd never say he didn't love me. He has to say, "Of course, I love you." By remembering his core feelings, he softens. The first brick in his wall comes down, and then they topple.

SEX

In the beginning, Joe wanted to have sex every single day, at least once, if not twice or three times. I was amazed by his appetite. Frankly, I couldn't keep up. If I didn't give it to him once a day, he'd get upset. That's when he told me about his severe poison condition. He described the need to expel his junk like it's a real physical crisis. We all know that Blue Ball Syndrome does not appear in any medical textbooks. But for Joe, not having enough sex is detrimental to his overall health. He genuinely can't function otherwise. He gets fidgety and stressed, distracted and irritable. He can't sleep, eat, or form complete sentences—I'm kidding, well, kind of.

Honestly, our sex impacts how we treat each other out of bed. If I put his papers in the wrong place, and we've had sex for the last five nights, it's cool. But if we hadn't had sex for the last five nights, it's not.

All men might not be as sexually voracious as Joe. But according to a poll of my friends, men do tend to need more sex than the women. Obviously, there are exceptions. The general consensus though is that if men don't get their minimum of sexual activity (on a sliding scale), they go crazy. Women can go a bit longer before bother and frustration set in.

The physical side of saying "no" to sex is only the beginning. What's even worse is the emotional game-playing that goes with it.

> When women brush off sex again and again, the man feels resentment. He gets sick of always initiating and getting shot down. He might understand that his wife is tired and busy with kids. But the rejection also makes him worry that she doesn't

want him. So he waits for her to come on to him, ready to go, to prove that she has the urge as badly as he does. He might hold out for a while to see how long it goes before she initiates. Meanwhile, she thinks, *He's the man. He should come get me.* The two of them are rolled over on their sides, purposefully not touching each other. It can go on for weeks, both refusing to give in. Their bed might as well be an iceberg.

If Melissa does one thing in this book to help women in their marriages, it should be to get them to initiate sex more often. Once every four or five times would be enough.

Men try to act like nothing bothers them, and they often succeed. They're so good at appearing strong and unflappable, women forget that men have insecurities, too. When women feel a crisis of desirability, they ask flat out, "How do I look?" Or they put on more makeup, buy a new outfit. Men do nothing. They act like nothing bothers them. In fact, a good indicator that your husband is upset is when he acts the most blasé. When Joe acts like nothings wrong, I get nervous.

Men need to know their wives want them or they feel insulted. Words aren't enough. Only actions will prove it beyond a shadow of doubt. He'll wait for you to make a move. Joe has done this. He's said to himself, "Let's see how many nights we'll go." If I don't initiate sex, it's because I'm exhausted. It has nothing to do with a lack of desire. But Joe takes it to heart. When three days go by and he hasn't touched me, I know he feels ignored. By day four, he starts violently tossing and turning in bed to make sure I get the message.

To prevent awkwardness, I reach over to him and touch his back or arm. It doesn't have to be a sexual touch per se. I spoon him from behind or kiss the back of his neck, just to show the love, that I care, that I noticed, and that I'm sorry. And that's pretty much all it takes. He turns around, and it's on.

> Refusing to initiate is a Top Three reason men cheat. The ugliest girl in the world could come on to a man in that state of mind, and he might have to go for it. He thinks, *At least* someone *wants me.*

When a person feels insulted, the knee-jerk reaction is to strike back. Withholding sex from each other will hurt, but neither partner wins by playing this game. How messed up is it to have the goal of making your spouse suffer? In any circumstances, if hurting your partner is the way to feel better about yourself, you might want to rethink your game plan. In my marriage, the goal is to love and support each other. If you go down the destructive road of purposefully pissing each other off or making him jealous, you'll both suffer for it.

Don't be stubborn and think, *He's such a baby.* Men need reassurance just like women do. So hug him, kiss him, show him the love, and he'll give in. A week's worth of resentment and tension are forgiven in fifteen minutes.

Growing up on the Jersey Shore. Seaside Heights boardwalk, 1982.

Dad and his four girls. My sisters are ten and twelve years older than me. Can you say, "accident?"

Toms River High School East, 1994. Joe would probably love it if I still wore this uniform.

Kim's wedding in 1989. Check out the poofy dress and headbands.

"Joe, will you marry me?"

The day I changed from Marco to Gorga, in 2004.

With my sisters, Lysa and Kim. *(Photo by Michael Simon)*

As close as we are, we are also so different. The dresses say it all. *(Photo by Manny Carabel/MTC Photography)*

My sisters and their hubbies are our best friends. How cool is that? *(Photo by Barbara Sage of Sage Photo Studios)*

When Joe sees red, he charges!

We love the shore! It's where we drop the cell phones and just spend quality time.

We love Halloween! I love finding over-the-top costumes for the kids. *(Photo by Michael Simon)*

My kids are my world—I was born to be a mommy. *(Portrait artistry by Linda Marie)*

Ciao! Te amo always. *(Portrait artistry by Linda Marie)*

CRITICISM

I'd been raised to be independent. I'd supported myself for years. I'd always dreamed of getting married and having gorgeous dark-haired Italian babies in a big stone house. I met Joe and got my wish. When we first got married, we still had to figure each other out. He wanted to set a precedent of how he wanted his wife to be. He flexed his muscles. His style was to make corrections and to teach me from the beginning days of our marriage exactly how he envisioned our life together. Joe always says, "You got to teach someone to walk straight on the knife. If you slip, you're going to get cut." Even if something didn't bother him that badly, he'd bring it up. He wanted to make sure that I knew, for example, if I ran out to CVS and he came home from work to an empty house, he didn't like it. He'd call me and say, "I don't care if you're out all day long. But I don't want to come home to an empty house."

Some of you ladies might be rolling your eyes over this and saying, "Screw you. If I need to go out, I'm going out." But I understood and respected his wishes. Instead of flexing my muscles and rolling my eyes, I went with it. He doesn't come home to an empty house, if I can help it. There are the simple things I'm talking about that make our marriage what it is. In a way, it's flattering that he wants me all the time.

My independent side wondered if he was trying to control me. I tried not to be too analytical about it. When he asked me, for example, not to clean up after dinner but to sit with him on the couch, I realized he just wanted to be together. It's not about control. If I expected him to support and protect our family, it seemed a small thing to greet him with a kiss when he came home for a long day at work, or hang on the couch at night. In a marriage, ego has to be chipped away. "Me" has to be replaced by "we." Instead of just pushing back, I understand him.

A lot of people don't even know what they want, or they're afraid to tell their spouses the honest truth. Joe's not a guy who doesn't speak up to his wife and then bitches about her behind her back. Even if Joe's comments are sometimes annoying, I'd rather him make them than feel like he can't express himself. I give him a lot of credit for saying what he feels. I always know what's going on in that head of his. He tells me to my face and it works.

HIS WEDDING BAND

Joe doesn't wear his ring. He says his fingers are too big, and that they swell up. He worries it'll catch on a nail when he's at work. He says he's claustrophobic with a ring on his finger. I used to give him a hard time about it. Wearing a ring is a sign that he's mine. If he went into a bar, a woman would see his naked finger and assume he was single. His argument is that, if he went to bar to hook up, he'd just take the ring off before he went in. And now, he's pretty well-known for being a married man, thanks to the show. He also says that women in bars are drawn to men wearing a band. Women are drawn to what they can't have. Maybe it's better that he doesn't wear it.

FAT LIPS

My girlfriend called me up one day from her doctor's office. She was getting her lips done. "Come over and try it!" she said. I was curious. I went over there. I didn't want huge big fake lips, so I got just a little done.

Mistake! Just that little bit made me look like a duck. I hadn't told Joe what I was up to. That night when I was cooking dinner, I kept my back to him so he wouldn't see my face.

He noticed, of course. And he was NOT happy. "You look disgusting! You're like one of those freaks from Beverly Hills! What are you doing to yourself? What are you turning into?" He started slamming the plastic tabletop on the high chair (obviously, the baby wasn't in it), and it cracked.

Fat lips tell no lies: I hated the look, too.

He didn't talk to me for two weeks, about as long as the bruising lasted. When they went back down to normal size, I was relieved, not only for his sake. Puffy lips just didn't feel right for me. Lesson learned. I never got them done again.

JEALOUSY

We both turn into a green-eyed monster on occasion. I insist on hiring all of Joe's secretaries at work. If the candidate is over sixty, with an eye patch, a hump and a bald spot, she's hired. I never want to see a twenty-three-year-old former Miss New Jersey within a hundred feet of his building. I purposefully hang photos of me and the kids all over his office walls to make sure any woman who comes through that door knows he's taken.

During a rough work period, Joe was so distracted, he lost interest in sex. He went for ten days without touching me. I suspected he was cheating and went nuts. I let my imagination get the better of me. Joe would never cheat. He wouldn't dare! The idea of another woman getting next to my man brings out the tiger in me. I'm a fighter. I'll cut the bitch who tries.

Joe is even worse than I am. When we were dating, we went to a restaurant with friends. One of the girls brought a guy who had a big tattoo on his arm. Joe and I don't have any tattoos. I just never had the urge to mark my skin. But when someone has a good one, I want a closer look. I asked to see this guy's ink. He rolled up his sleeve. I touched the tattoo and said, "I like it."

Joe went insane, throwing back his chair, jumping up, screaming at me to get my hands off of that guy. It was so embarrassing and infuriating. We were in a crowded restaurant. I touched a guy's arm. Big deal! We left before we finished eating, both of us in a rage. This was the first time I thought, *"Whoa! He's old-school Italian!"* This was why my mother said, "Never marry an Italian."

Later that night after we stopped yelling, he explained, "You can't touch a stranger's arm and say how much you like it. It was like you were flirting with him in front of all those people." And so on.

I wasn't flirting or gushing about tattoos. That was all Joe's interpretation of what I thought was harmless acknowledgment of some guy's body art. But if I reversed the situation, and Joe asked a woman to lift up her sleeve so he could stroke her bare arm and said how much he liked it, I would've flipped over the table. New rule in our relationship: No touching other people's arms. I'm not saying it has to be a rule in everyone's marriage. But in ours, it's set in stone.

FORGIVE AND REMEMBER

. . . .

I laughed out loud when I read about a study that said if wives forgive and forget their husband's bad behavior too quickly, the husbands go right back to making the same mistakes again. If the wife forgives, the husband forgets what he did wrong. The study said that wives should remain a little bit angry to reinforce how he messed up. Since a husband will do just about anything to get out of the doghouse, he'll learn his lesson if she stays mad.

THE BATTLES NOT CHOSEN

Some classic couples fights just don't set off sparks for Joe and me. Including:

CONTROL OF THE REMOTE

I couldn't believe a recent *Vanity Fair* poll that said the number one thing couples fight over is control of the remote. Seriously? It seems like an argument from the "clicker" era. Now everyone has a cell phone, iPad, computer or another TV. Just go into another room and watch a different show. Or TiVo your favorite show and watch it later when he's at work, in the garage, or goes into the bathroom with a magazine. Or how about this: Turn the TV off and talk to each other?

When relaxing in the evening, I like to be in the same room with Joe, usually my kids are running in circles around the house. It's our time together. Slinking off to another room to watch my shows would defeat the purpose. But I'm not going to push my TV agenda on him. I have my nights that are must-see TV and Joe can't claw the remote out of hand. But I give in on Sunday and Monday nights. We're always ready for some football. No matter what else is on, that's one thing he won't budge on. I don't even try.

I know a lot of husbands claim that the *Real Housewives* shows are torture to their nerves. It physically pains them to watch—yet they all run up to me on the street and tell me what I did last week on the show. "My wife makes me watch it," they say, embarrassed to admit they like it. Sometimes, men want you to take control of the remote.

PARENTING

Joe and I are of one mind about how to raise our kids. I don't think we've ever fought over parenting philosophy. We share the same values about family, we have the same dreams and expectations for our kids. We agree on punishments, chores, and homework hours. We'll see how it goes when they get older, but we have talked about a lot of scenarios. (For more on parenting, skip a couple chapters ahead.)

THE IN-LAWS

Do Joe and I have conflicts related to our families? Uh, *yeah*. But we don't let those issues come between us. When things get hot, we remind each other that it's all noise. It's a sandstorm. But in the middle of the storm, with the sand swirling around us, we stand together solid as a rock. There's family that you're born into. And there's the family you choose. We'd probably argue a lot more about our relatives if we didn't share that core belief. Our nuclear family (husband, wife, children) is the center of our universe. We would move heaven and earth to protect that.

HOW TO DISMANTLE A MARRIAGE BOMB

Rules for disengagement:

DON'T BLINK

To make your point, you have to look him in the eye. Other-wise, you can't be sure he's listening to you. Your words won't have the same raw power. Sell your point with your eyes. Use them to communicate sincerity and to be taken seriously. Unwavering eye contact—really *staring*—is the test to a couple's comfort level. If you can sustain it for the entire conversation, then you have the essential trust that marriage requires. If you find yourself looking away, then it begs the question, *How much do you really mean it?* If your husband drops his gaze, you have to wonder, *What's going on with him?* I'm not saying a break in eye contact means he's lying. But something about the exchange makes him uncomfortable.

WAIT IT OUT

I get over fights fairly quickly. Joe is the Incredible Sulk. He might stay mad for days over nothing. To him, though, it's something. He takes any conflict to heart because we love each other so much. I guess I'm just not as sensitive as he is. I used to let his sulking get to me. That face can really kill a good mood. But now I know to just let his emotions run their course. He'll come around eventually.

EASY DOES IT

Although I have been known to throw my phone at him (I got mad because he was mad for no reason), I usually just hurl words. You don't have to damage property to win. Words can do plenty of damage on their own. I'm witty to get my way. I'm sarcastic. If he yells and I say, "That's fascinating, Joe," or "You're a real tough guy," he gets crazy. If you push me, I'll come back louder than a police siren. But when I stay calm and use my words to argue a point, I tend to get my way. I make him realize that he's overreacting, and then he scales back to match me.

DON'T TAKE IT PERSONALLY

This is especially effective when Joe brings his work stress home with him. If someone ripped Joe off that day, he comes home a different person. If he gets one ounce of flack from me, he flips a switch and goes off. I know it's not really about me, so I don't get riled up. I suppose I could get angry back at him for getting the bulk end of his problems. But then again, that's what a spouse is for. You get to release your stress on someone you trust, who you know won't hold it against you. He'd like to yell at a colleague, client, or employee. But he yells at me and doesn't screw up a business deal. I can take it. Men's attitudes are determined by their work and finances. If their finances are off, look out. I've learned not to take it personally. It's not me, it's work. When I have a bad day at the "office," my reaction is to cry on Joe's shoulder. We have different styles of coping. We don't expect each other to change, but just to recognize how we each deal with work and money anxiety differently.

WHEN YOU LOSE, YOU WIN

Confidence is great. We all need it to succeed. I feel confident in who I am and what I can do. When I remind myself of that, it's less important to win a fight with Joe. Losing an argument doesn't take away who I am as a person. Having that perspective does make it a little easier to see an argument for what it is, and to understand Joe's side of it. Make no mistake. I still like to win. But there are times when Joe is right. Lose the ego.

CUT THE TENSION

At the tail end of a battle, humor helps. After the initial shouting match, Joe sometimes slips into teacher mode when he explains how he'd like to tweak my behavior. I know my husband like a book. When I'm in for a lesson, I sit back and listen. He needs to say what he has to say, and for me to agree. So I "yes" him to death. "Yes, Joe. Yes, honey. Yes, baby." I just keep repeating it. After a while, we both crack up.

GO OUT WITH A BANG

Make-up sex! The best way to put an argument to rest. You both lay down your weapons and declare yourselves victorious. No question, make-up sex is super charged. All that tension is released. You let down your guard completely and just get into it. Sometimes, during the make-up sex, he says, "I hate you! Oh, but you feel so good. I hate you. But I love you so much!" I just crack up.

LET IT GO

Sometimes, there's no solution to an argument. You have to be willing to say, "We're not going to solve this. Give me a kiss, let's watch a movie, and forget it."

MARRIAGE CONFIDENTIAL

. . . .

Everyone needs to vent to a sympathetic third party. Having an impartial sounding board has helped me understand Joe and myself better when emotions run high. When I need to confide in someone, I turn to the women I trust the most in the world—my mother and my sisters. I call up Lysa or Kim and say, "I'm furious at Joe!" and they can always talk me off the ledge.

Even with my sisters, I hold back a little bit. As much as I need to unload, there's a limit to the details I'll reveal. You never know. A massive blow up might peter out and turn into nothing the next day. But if I go to my sister and we spend an hour hashing it over, I'd feel embarrassed when she checked in and I say, "Oh, that blew over. It's nothing." Also, if you say too much, they might think differently about your marriage or husband. No matter how close an ally, your confidant is not in the marriage with you. She only hears one perspective, and it's biased. You might portray your husband as a monster, and that's what she'll believe regardless of whether it's the absolute truth.

I struggle with the impulse to reach out to my sisters the second after a fight. I'm an impulsive person. I really have to sit on my hands. But it's always better to wait one day before you make that call. See if it blows over. See how much you actually care the next morning. If an issue lingers for a few days, then it's wise to gather opinions, weigh them, and use them as a tool to fix things with your husband. A tool. Not a weapon. Don't bludgeon him by saying, "Well, my friends agree with me." The idea is to gain insight into yourself. Choose a confidant with high emotional intelligence. If you just want to hear your own words parroted back, then you might as well talk to the mirror.

THINK LONG TERM

I just saw this movie *Parental Guidance*. It was a great family movie. The Bette Midler character explains to her daughter why she always takes her husband's side. She says something along the lines of, "You kids grew up and left. My husband is the one who stayed. He's standing by me, and I'm standing by him."

That really stuck with me. Divorce is not an option. We are in it for the long haul. Our kids will move out one day. But Joe and I are here to stay. We'll probably have the same fights. And I'm a hundred percent fine with it. I'd be lost without our marriage. Every day, I envision our future, when the kids move out, and then come home for visits. When their rooms are filled up with their own children, our grandchildren. I can see us getting old (but staying hot). And I like what I see. A few fights here and there are nothing in terms of a whole life together. Seeing the big picture puts little arguments into perspective.

CHAPTER TEN

Kitchen Table Conversations

Joe and I got engaged the same year I graduated college and got my B.A. in elementary education. I went to a job fair and was hired at my very first interview. When I went home and told Joe, he said, "If you want to be a teacher, you can be the best one out there. But I'd love for you to work with me and build my company. I'm going to hate your having a boss. When I want you to go on vacation with me, I don't want someone to tell you that you can't."

The decision was totally up to me. I'd worked hard and earned my teaching degree. I had a job offer. I'd always wanted to run my own show, and earn my own money. That was the dream, and it was all falling into place. But at some point along the way, the dream changed. Teaching no longer felt like the right path. Something in my heart told me to help build the company with Joe for the sake of our future children. I went to work with my husband at his extremely successful landscaping business as a bookkeeper, secretary, and all-around whatever-needs-doing employee. I stayed there throughout my first pregnancy with Antonia, and in a limited basis for a couple of years after. By working in the company, I learned the business from the inside. I met the people. I understood what it was Joe did all day. Having a grasp of what your man does is crucial for any wife, and vice versa.

His business started out as landscape construction. During our ten years together, it grew from flipping two-family homes, to building custom homes, to buying old warehouses and converting them into the buildings we own today. Together, we expanded it into an extremely successful real estate development company. At first, the projects were small. But before long, they got bigger. He hired more employees, and I became a full-time housewife.

In the fall of 2008, I vividly remember Joe coming home from work one day and saying, "All our money is tied up. You can't spend an extra dollar this month."

Gino was a newborn. Antonia was two. The last month, I'd gone on a spending spree and dropped $10,000. But this month, he gave me a $100 to last all week. It didn't make sense. I was young, living in a large house, driving a Range Rover, with only $100 for groceries? I thought, *Why are you doing this?*

Was he putting a leash on me, or teaching me a lesson for spending too much the month before? It didn't make sense.

A lot of people have the misconception that Melissa and I are a Cinderella story. Not true at all. We've struggled. During the Recession, we went through hell. In 2008, four years after we got married, the real estate market crashed. I'd recently closed on one of the biggest projects I'd ever done. I came away from that with $2,000,000 and immediately reinvested it in thirty-eight homes being built on spec—meaning, houses to sell on completion. The real estate market dried up in New Jersey overnight. The value of my spec houses dropped in half. I didn't have cash to finish building them, and I lost every deal. All of the money I'd put into those properties was gone. Vanished.

Gino was born. When I left the hospital with Melissa and the baby, I had only $3,000 left in our account. No bank would give me a loan. I couldn't get any deals going without hard money. I had to go to a loan shark to borrow $50,000, with no money coming in. I made a budget, and would go down to barely enough gas in the truck to drive home.

That day I gave Melissa $100 and said, "No more for a week." That bill was all the money I had. If she told me she needed another $5 for milk, I couldn't give it to her. Our only glitch was when she questioned me about it. But then we sat down and talked it through. She was in the baby bubble, and wasn't aware what was going on out there. She had to learn about the economic downturn in a hurry, the hard way.

This is how we survived: Every market was going down, but scrap metal prices were going through the roof. I bought a big warehouse with radiators throughout the building. Every morning, I'd have my guys cut the metal, fill up the truck and sell it for $1,700. I'd take that money to buy Sheetrock and paint to keep the warehouse renovation going. I'd pay the guys, and keep $100 to give to Melissa.

My refrain was always, "We'll get through this. As long as I've got my two arms and two legs, I'll keep fighting." I worked at reviving the business. My hours were long. She spent a lot of time alone at home with two babies. She didn't give me grief about being home alone. She proved to be the woman she is. I never had anxiety about staying at work or felt pressure about running home to my wife. She never complained.

Our credit cards were all maxed out. Melissa called me and said, "I need diapers." I picked her up and we went to Costco. I had $79 on me. I gave Melissa a fifty and waited in the truck with the kids. She got a huge package for $40, and went to the register to pay.

The cashier said, "Your membership ended last month. I need $100 to renew it."

Melissa called me in the truck and said, "I need another hundred."

I didn't have it.

"What should I do?" she asked.

"Just come out."

Melissa hung up, and just left the store. She didn't say a word about it. We went straight to ShopRite and paid the same amount for a little box of diapers.

This was our life every day for three years. It took thirty years off my life. If I hadn't pulled out every stop and used every trick in the book, we would have lost everything. Other developers went bankrupt and killed themselves. We kept it together. Our accounts were empty some weeks. But I still managed to come up with the mortgage each month.

We finished the warehouse. I convinced some bankers to come to the site to meet me and see the place. Fifteen people came by. They watched me work. I told them my story, and made my pitch. I had one shot to prove myself. At that time, banks were locked down tight. But somehow, I sold them on my company. At the end of the day, the main guy pulled me over said, "Let's do business." It was a watershed moment. After that, I got another bank on board, and they gave me a major loan. I'd walk into a boardroom in dirty jeans and work boots. They're all straight edge in suits. I'd crack some jokes and get them laughing. I got my loans based on my personality. I was able to buy a second building, and a third. Relief doesn't begin to explain how it felt. We were okay. We'd survived it. Before long, we were better than ever.

During those nightmare three years, not once did Melissa complain, give me a look, or imply in any way that our struggle was my fault. I give her a ton of credit. She never tried to keep up with the Joneses or compared me to anyone else. She cut back. She never made me feel like a loser or looked at me like a failure. A lot of women with two babies would have lost faith or patience. But she believed in me. She stood by me. I went to work like a machine, like an animal. I had to get it done for my family at home.

It was a rough time. Joe was not happy. We went from having no worries to stressing over every dollar. Leading up to it, I had a tough pregnancy with Gino. I was extremely moody. My progesterone levels were off the charts, and I was put on bedrest for twelve weeks before the delivery. To go from that straight into the recession was mind-boggling.

He trusted me to tell me the truth. We were flat broke. I didn't make him feel like less of a man because of it. I don't react like a spoiled housewife. We looked each other in the eye, discussed the matter, and worked together for a common cause—the security of our family. We watched the news and read the papers. It helped to know we weren't the only ones affected. The recession pummeled the state of New Jersey, the whole country, and the world. It wasn't Joe's fault, and there wasn't a lot he could do to fix our situation. Still, the sudden change was hard to accept. We went from flush to bust practically overnight. It felt like the rug was pulled out from under me. After a stumble, I found my feet. *Okay*, I thought. *I can make do with less. I can make do with next to nothing.* I'd done it as a student, and I could manage again. But, this time, I wasn't alone. The reason I didn't look at Joe like he was a loser was because I was in awe of him. He never wavered, never stopped busting ass. I saw ruin all around me, but Joe was pure energy, pure drive. He pulled us back up by sheer force of will.

In hindsight, I'm glad we went through that experience. We were in the trenches together. Faith in each other kept both of us going. That was a big "win" for us. We recovered as a team. It's not how you act in the good times that demonstrate your character. It's how you act when the chips are down that shows who you are. Our chips were *way* down. They were gone! We came out of it both humbled and with greater confidence in our ability to withstand just about anything.

What doesn't kill a marriage only makes it stronger.

There are no financial secrets between us. We are an open book, and our books are wide open. We're partners in marriage and business. We have a joint checking and savings account. Joe reads all of the contracts related to my career. It's not possible to hide money (or the lack of it) from each other, or for us to spend without the other knowing about it. I write the checks and pay all the bills in this house. I oversee the books for his business. Obviously, Joe has a staff that manages his buildings and accounts. But no one looks out for him as much as I do. And no one looks out for me like Joe does.

FAMILY FINANCE ITALIAN STYLE

I can't speak for all Italian marriages here. But Joe and I have sorted out the way we operate.

COMPROMISE

Joe and I do disagree about what to spend our money on. I always want to do more stuff around the house. Lately, for obvious reasons, I've been looking into beefing up our home security. I want cameras in *every* corner. But Joe says, "For what? We don't need it." So we compromise. He gets me my cameras and I'll buy four pairs of shoes instead of five.

KNOWLEDGE IS POWER

Family finance discussions are ongoing. It's not a conversation you can have once and consider it over and done with. The money talk never stops because the bills keep coming. The mood of the discussion fluctuates, just like your income. It's wise to brace for some unpleasantness. As much as you might want to bury your head in the sand, you can't ignore the financial health of the household. You have to face it head on. It might seem like a huge relief to just let your husband deal with it all, but ignorance is not bliss. Personally, I'd go crazy if I didn't now what was going on with something crucial to our children's future. I need to know how we're doing for my peace of mind.

LIVE AS WELL AS YOU CAN

Buy the best car you can afford. Stretch by buying a house in the nicest neighborhood with the best schools. Buy the classics, a fur coat you'll wear for thirty years. If you're going to splurge on a pair of shoes, buy the black pumps you'll wear a hundred times. You'll always look rich if you buy the best classics you can afford. When you have extra cash around, then go for the trends.

> Melissa and I don't fight over purchases. I gave her credit cards. She respected them. She knows her limits. I've always been lucky that she's good that way. It's not so easy for other guys. If she goes overboard, like at Christmas time, I say, "Calm down." We've never had the fight where I've confronted her with a crumbled up credit card bill in my hand, shaking it in air. Nothing like that. She's a born saver, just like I am. Don't get me wrong. I'm sure she's snuck up the stairs with a shopping bag when my back was turned. I know all you women do that.

DON'T SPEND EVERY PENNY

If the last five years in our nation's history have taught me anything, it's that you can't live the high life and spend every penny that comes in. It's easy to fall into that trap. A lot of people did, and when the recession hit in 2008, they were crushed financially. Money is not a given. When it runs out, marriages can take a sharp downturn as well. The tendency is to look around for someone to blame. A lot of people wind up pointing the finger at those closest to you. The number one cause of divorce is money trouble. Don't let that green stuff get the best of you. Saving money might save your marriage one day.

Our only money argument is that Melissa wants to buy me nice clothes. I work in construction. I get filthy. I live in jeans and T-shirts. For going out, I already have a few good suits and shirts. They're all I'll ever need. But Melissa loves fashion. She tells me she wants to buy me a $400 bathing suit. I say, "You're crazy!" I'll wear a Polo suit. I don't care. But then I go out and get her a $400 bathing suit. I'd rather see her in it.

TWO INCOMES

I went from being a housewife who needed to go to my husband for money, to being out in the world, getting paychecks, and having my own work appointments and a packed schedule. Before the show, I never needed help with the kids and, if I did, I'd hire a babysitter. But all of a sudden, I had to ask Joe, "Can you help me out?" It's a lot with the kids. I don't know how much longer I can go without getting someone in the house to help. I'll go as long as I can without doing that and rely on Joe, my mother, and sisters before I buckle. Joe loves his children and spending time with them. But he does resent the idea that their mother isn't available to them 24/7.

It was an adjustment. For years, I was the one making money. I paid for everything and Melissa took care of the house and the kids. That was our

> life. Then suddenly, I'm earning, and I'm paying for the recording studio, and for her songs, and for her choreographer, and the hair and makeup, and then she asked me take phone calls for her, and to stay home with the kids so she could do an appearance somewhere. What happened to our normal life as a married couple? I thought I was a big real estate guy. Am I seriously turning into my wife's assistant?

The saying is, "Money changes everything." But for us, it wasn't my income that caused problems, but my career. It took Joe a good year before our new lifestyle became the new normal. Now we're in the third year, and he's accepted the fact that I'm working. I love that I'm also contributing to the life the kids will have one day. In the long run, it's all for them.

ONE POT

In this house, when my check arrives, I hand it to Joe. It goes into our joint account, the only one we have. I'd never keep it separate, and think of it as "mine." God knows, he's never considered his money "his." He shared his home with me before we married and since, he's supported me generously. Every dollar that comes into this household belongs to all of us. Our money is "ours." Separate accounts and credit card statements just open the door for secrets and lies. Not that Joe and I would have anything to hide from each other. But we can't, and won't. Knowing we can't doesn't feel restrictive. It actually creates a sense of freedom. Neither of us tells the other what we can't do.

If I see a large chunk taken out of the account, I ask, and he tells me. The only thing he asks me about, is to be careful when I'm at the mall. I splurge on clothes.

You could be billionaires, but without trust your marriage isn't worth a dime.

God willing, my children will not have to work three jobs to get through college. Joe and I are in sync about that. We want to make their lives easier than we had it, but not too easy! They understand the value of hard work, and they'll have summer jobs and work at Joe's office one day. We expect them all to go to college. But if the boys decide they want to go into the business with Joe (Gorga & Sons does have a nice ring to it), Joe and I will discuss it and decide what to do. No doors are closed. No decisions are made. The future is a mystery. Whatever it might bring, though, we are united in our desire to help our kids be successful and give them every advantage.

CHAPTER ELEVEN

· ·

Good Homekeeping

Before *Housewives*, I used to come home to find
Melissa at the stove, the house spotless, the kids
running around. We'd kiss, eat, put the kids to bed
and I'd have my time alone with her. It was the best

part of my day, what I lived for. Then, she got on the show. All of the sudden, she was going here and there, spending more time away, on the phone, on the computer. This was my biggest objection to the show. It wasn't having hairdressers and film crews in my house, or becoming a target for haters online, or even having to deal with personal situations on camera. I missed having Melissa all to myself.

I know Joe misses that. But, the truth is, it's partially his fault. We made this decision together.

My number one life dream was to have a passionate, loving marriage and raise happy, healthy children. Family is the top priority. My number two dream was to be a professional singer/songwriter. It started when I was six-years-old, performing for my father and seeing him smile when I sang and danced on the coffee table. When you get so much positive feedback for doing something you love, you get hooked on the idea of doing it on a larger scale.

I associated singing with my father. After he died, though, the positive feelings turned dark. Even singing along with the radio reminded me of the car accident, and that I'd never see my father smile at me again. It was too painful. For years, I didn't so much as hum a tune.

When I had Antonia, I started singing her lullabies and little songs to comfort her when she was upset. She always smiled when I sang, and it reminded me of my father. It was bittersweet. Freeing my vocal cords again was a huge relief.

I hadn't realized how much I'd missed using them. But it killed me that my father never got to meet my baby. In time, Gino and Joey also responded to my voice. But none of my children loved it as much as my husband.

One night, while I was singing the kids to sleep, Joe said, "I love it when you sing. You have an amazing voice. You should do something with that."

I brushed it off. I wasn't sure I could handle singing for anyone but our family. And then, Joe stunned me by building a recording studio in our basement. He was determined that I should follow my passion. But also, he wanted me to push past the pain I associated with singing. Joe is empathic. What hurts me destroys him. He feels powerless when he can't take away my sorrow, so he tried to help me come to terms with it.

Building the recording studio, in a way, was Joe painting me into a corner. I couldn't *not* sing now, after all the work he did. As soon as I accepted that I was going to sing—on camera—I couldn't wait to get started.

Now when I do it, I honor my father. I still ache from missing him. I can summon the happy memories without sinking into the negative. Joe's encouragement helped me to reconnect with my father. The most appropriate way to thank him was to write a ballad called "How Many Times" that expresses my gratitude and love. Fans liked what they heard, and the song rose to number four on the iTunes charts.

That's why it's ironic when Joe sometimes complains about my newfound success and not being home all the time anymore. He helped put me there. He's the inspiration and the reason I've been so fortunate. My greatest fortune has been marrying the one man who would push me to chase my bliss, even at the expense of his own. He was probably kicking himself for doing it! But his original impulse was to push me to make something of myself.

What does all this have to do with my being a good home-keeper? Well, before *Housewives*, I was a housewife. No matter how far the show or my singing takes me, I'm still a housewife first and foremost. Fame is a distant second. If my career ever compromised my marriage, I'd give it up in a heartbeat. If I had to make a choice between being at home or sitting on top of the world, I'd lock all the doors and barricade myself inside these walls. There's no happiness without Joe and the kids. All the success in the world would be meaningless if I didn't have my sanctuary to come back to and my family to share it with.

Having hit songs will not keep me warm at night. Joe will.

When Joe and I met, I was a struggling student. He was a local businessman. We weren't TV personalities with even the faintest notion of being famous. We were everyday people. We still are. The routine of making dinner and keeping a clean house is how I stay grounded. It keeps me humble. I don't exist in a fame/ego bubble. I spend eighty percent of my life at home. I'm proud of it, and I work hard to keep it looking beautiful.

People don't believe me, but I do all the day-to-day cleaning of our house. Twice a month, a housekeeper comes over to help with major scrubbing. Between her visits, if the kids make a mess in the kitchen, I break out the Lysol. I have an obsession with vacuuming. My OCD sets in, and after I do one room, I go through the whole house. I do take a lot of pride in how well I maintain our house. It's a big place. If I can walk through the rooms, glancing around, everything in its place, I feel calm and relieved.

Does Joe help? Uh, not on your life! I could hold a grudge

that he has never once scoured a lasagne dish, but my philosophy about that is . . .

DON'T CRY OVER IT

If there's spilled milk on the floor, Joe'll walk by it five times without once picking up a sponge. I used to ask, "Are you going to keep ignoring that spill or clean it?"

He says, "Nope."

Someone might look at Joe and think, "Chauvinist pig." He sounds like one sometimes! They might look at me and think, "Throwback." The way I see it, Joe is cleaning up messes at work all day long—things you can't wipe up with a sponge. That's his job. It's my job to clean up spilled milk. I just do it. There is simply no point to arguing about something that requires all of five seconds of my time, and next to zero energy.

THE ZEN OF HOMEKEEPING

Women are multitaskers. Cleaning can be soul nurturing and creatively productive, if you use it that way. Anyone can fold laundry on automatic pilot. So while I go through my chores, I try to write song lyrics, or meditate, or think of chapter ideas for this book. My life is my inspiration. If I can find the Zen in changing the sheets, then anyone can.

HOW MANY GORGAS DOES IT TAKE
TO CHANGE A LIGHTBULB?

We had a huge fight once over whether or not Joe would change a lightbulb. It was in the kitchen in a ceiling fixture twenty feet up. To change this bulb, you'd have to get the ladder from the garage, carry it halfway through the house, climb it, replace the bulb, and take the ladder back to the garage. Seemed like man's work to me. So when he came home at 8:30 P.M., I asked him to do it.

He refused. "I put in a twelve-hour day. I'm tired. If you don't want to do it yourself, hire someone."

Begin heated argument. I told him I worked hard, too, that it'd be a crazy to hire a workman to change a freakin' lightbulb. But he said that when he came home after working all day, he wanted to get on the floor and play with the kids. He wanted to get in bed and play with me. Refusing to do a simple task seemed like a bizarre line to draw. For Joe, it all comes down to respect. He was offended that I'd want him to waste even twenty minutes of our time together on a chore. Actually, Joe doesn't want me to do chores either when he got home in the evenings.

I asked myself, "Do I want the bulb changed more than I want my husband to bond with the kids or shower me with affection?"

Screw the lightbulb.

Someone's got to give. I could get mad and push, or I could accept his wishes and calm down. We wound up having a peaceful dinner together—with mood lighting, although it was a bit hard to see the food—and a beautiful night.

So, how many Gorgas *does* it take to change a lightbulb?

None. The next day, Joe sent over one of his workers to change every bulb in the house.

DO YOU REALLY WANT TO SEE YOUR MAN ON HIS KNEES NEXT TO A BUCKET OF SUDSY WATER?

In theory, men sharing household chores is great. I've heard women say, "Nothing is as sexy as watching my man do the dishes after dinner." When I hear that, I think, *Um, I can think of about a thousand things that are sexier that that!* A man doing the dishes does not turn me on. Talk about crushing the fantasy of his being the big, bad protector. A man cutting down a tree with a chain saw, now that might flip my switch. Anyway, a study came out recently that pretty much confirmed my belief. It said that couples who stick to traditional gender role chore division have more sex. Couples where the man does typical "feminine" chores have less sex. I can tell you why. When gender roles are confused, sexual roles are, too. If he's at the sink and then changing diapers, then who throws who down in the bed? In our marriage, Joe is always the man, doing masculine things (except when he dressed as Snooki on Halloween). I'm the woman, and I do the female things, including housework.

DRIVING MS. GORGA

· · · · · · · · · · · · · ·

If a man needs a maid (to quote John Lennon), a woman needs a chauffeur. Joe is my driver. It would be hilarious if I got him some white gloves and a patent leather cap. Joe always rushes to open the door for me. He helps me get into my seat, and closes the door. If I have bags or boxes, he puts them in the trunk or backseat. Then he gets in and drives me wherever I want to go. It makes me feel sexy to be treated like a lady.

He wouldn't have it any other way, not only because he likes being a gentleman. He thinks I'm the worst driver in the world. But it's a known fact that he's a terrible driver. He gets pulled over a few times a month, and I never do (well, hardly ever). But he says he's a nervous wreck when I drive, especially on the highway. I change lanes, and he starts yelling, "Watch out!" On a ten-hour trip, he wanted to drive the whole way. Then I'm a wreck. The kids and I get stomachaches, and nauseous. Antonia complains, "I don't feel good!" I make him pull over. Then I drive.

ONLY LOSERS KEEP SCORE

A marriage is not a competitive sport. As soon as you start thinking of it as a running tally of chores and obligations, you'll never feel like he's doing enough for you, and vice versa. That attitude is toxic. It's the opposite of romance. Back when you started dating, your objective, and his, was to do as much as you could to make each other happy. If each person does whatever he can for the family, it will inspire the other to do as much as she can. Saying, "I took the garbage out five times last week, what have you done for me lately?" will inspire your partner to do the bare minimum to hit his benchmarks, and nothing more, or he'll be so resentful, he'll passive aggressively do nothing. Keep counting chores, and the days of your marriage are numbered.

CHAPTER TWELVE

· ·

Princess and Princes of the Castle

My kids! Love them to death. Joe and I are the King and Queen of the house, Antonia is our princess, and Gino and Joey are the little princes. We want to give our children everything, but in moderation without overindulging. The kids stay up a little later than they should—okay a lot later than they should—but otherwise Joe wouldn't get enough time to play with them. We're teaching them respect, loyalty, honesty, and hard work. Upholding the Italian tradition, we gave them family names. Antonia Rose, age eight, was named after my mother-in-law and my father. Gino

Anthony, age six, was named after my father-in-law Giancarlo. And Giuseppe Marco (Joey), age three, was named after my husband. Everything we do, we do for them. We work for their security. We live for their happiness. Before Joe and I met, he put $200,000 into a college savings account for his future children. Family came first for him, even before he had one.

Joe and I got pregnant right away after our wedding. We wanted to. Sometimes, we look back and think about what it would have been like to have more time with just the two of us. But we don't regret the decision to get pregnant right away. We're both such family oriented people. Joe had been missing an extended family his whole life. His parents came from Italy. He didn't have any cousins or aunts and uncles in New Jersey. They were all back in the old country. I'd dreamed of being part of a perfect family with a daddy that came home every night, a mommy who put dinner on the table, talked to the neighbors over the fence and baked cookies for her kids. I wanted that fantasy to start ASAP.

We were shooting to conceive in the fall for a summer baby. No guesswork needed. I can feel it when I ovulate. I said to Joe, "Let's make a baby tonight" or "Come home, I'm ovulating." Bam, first month of trying, I got knocked up with Antonia. I'm a fertile Myrtle. Same thing with the boys, too.

Getting pregnant was easy. Being pregnant wasn't such a snap. I had problems with my hormone levels. They caused severe mood swings. I was on bed rest for months with Gino. That was the worst. Because of some complicating factors, I had planned Caesarian sections for all my deliveries. Since I could choose the date, we picked August 12 for Antonia, and September 12 for Gino. We tried, but couldn't work the magic of twelve for Joey. He was born on April 27.

For all our pregnancies, we decided to wait until the birth to know the gender. The first time, Melissa was holding the baby pointed out and to the front, which supposedly meant "boy." The old wive's tale also said if the mother gains a lot of weight, she's carrying a girl. She only gained 22 pounds. It was nothing. I was convinced we were having a boy. My sister had two girls. Our cousins had girls. I *really* wanted a boy.

So I was in the operating room with Melissa at the birth. The doctors were cutting her open. That was scary to watch. She got an epidural and didn't feel it. But I almost fainted. I had to walk out of the room, take a few deep breaths, and then come back. I got in there with the video camera, and I described to Melissa what was happening. I was afraid about having a girl. I know how I can be. I'd be insanely jealous of any boy coming around for my daughter. Having a boy would be so much easier.

The doctor reached in, and pulled out Antonia. The old wives were wrong. I stood there in shock looking at my baby girl.

It was the most incredible, beautiful moment of my life.

Melissa started crying. I started crying. I nearly dropped the camera.

I'd never seen Joe cry before. When his first child was being born, he cried like a baby. And then he broke out in hives.

I counted Antonia's fingers and toes, and immediately felt itchy. The nurse and doctors were poking my daughter with needles, and bending her arm back to get blood. I had a fight with the nurse. I said, "She's an infant! You're too rough!"

The nurse said, "Excuse me, we do this all the time."

(As it is, I don't think the doctor liked me much. When I went to a pregnancy checkup with Melissa, the doctor wanted to see if she was dilated, and inserted a finger to examine her. I said, "Ohh, I'm jealous." Melissa turned red. She was so embarrassed. Oops. The doctor pretended she didn't hear me.)

The sight of them handling my baby like that freaked me out so much, I started itching all over my body.

Melissa, still on the operating table, saw what was happening. I was scratching like I had poison ivy. She needed rest so she told me to go home and take a shower. I didn't want to leave her, but the itching was crazy. I drove home and saw I had red lumps all over my ass, my back, and up and down my arms.

"What the hell is that?" I yelled. I'd never seen anything like it before. I drove right back to the hospital and showed it to a nurse.

"You've got hives," she said.

I saw my daughter being born, and was so amazed and nervous, I broke out in hives! I realized that the bumps would go away. But being a

> nervous father was just how life was going to be from now on. I'd see Antonia in a pink outfit, and break out in hives again. She was my baby. I was responsible for her. The nervous feeling was so huge, my body reacted against it.

We had Gino two years later. That pregnancy was my worst. When the time came to deliver, I was ready to meet my baby and end twelve weeks of bed rest. Just like all parents, we prayed for a healthy baby. I would have been happy with either gender. I got my girl with Antonia. But Joe wanted a boy pretty badly. I had my fingers crossed.

> When we had Gino, I went crazy. My first son. I was so happy. In the delivery room, I was yelling, "It's a boy! It's a boy!"
>
> I asked the nurse, "Is that a big one? Normal? Is he big for his age?" I looked down at him and thought, "That's my boy!" I put a Giants jersey on him right away.
>
> Around seven or eight months later, Melissa and I woke up one night to the sound of Gino coughing. It was 3:00 A.M. He was in a crib in our room, struggling to take breaths between loud barking coughs. Melissa and I had no idea what was going on. We flipped out. What was this? What do we do? We raced to the hospital. Melissa

was holding Gino, trying to keep it together while he cried his eyes out.

We went to St. Joseph's Hospital's emergency room. They examined Gino and diagnosed him with croup. It's a viral infection that narrows the upper airways, making it nearly impossible to breathe, and is more common in boys than girls. He had a bad case, and had to stay in the hospital. We were destroyed. Seeing a tiny baby cough like that tears your heart out.

He stayed on the pediatric intensive care for three days. We never left the hospital. The ward was for really sick kids. Some of them had cancer. Melissa and I looked at each other and said, "We are blessed with what we have."

At that point in time, things were going on with my family. Let's just say some of them were giving Melissa a hard time. She was unhappy about it, and I did what I could to calm her down and make things smoother. At Gino's hospital bed, I looked at my wife, and thought, *It's me and her right now. My life is this woman.* I already knew that logically. We were married and had two children. But being with her there, and seeing how brave she was brought me that much closer to her. Dealing with a crisis took our trust and respect to a whole new level.

My mother came to the hospital. Her mother came. Our family was supportive. But we were the parents. Only the two of us were there around the clock together. Her strength never wavered. It made me want to be strong for her.

After five days (it seemed like five months), Gino recovered. He could breathe normally again. We left with medicine and a nebulizer. It's been five years. Gino still gets croup, but we know how to handle it now. That whole experience was terrifying. A real trial by fire. We came out in one solid piece.

When Gino had croup, it was the scariest five days of my life. He was less than a year old. I wouldn't leave him for five minutes. I wore the same clothes for days. He had tubes in him. Any mother who sees her child connected to machines understands the agony of it. My son was just sitting there, helpless. He was so tiny. As serious as his condition was, he was one of the healthiest kids in the pediatric ward. You'd walk through the halls and see babies in hospital gowns. Some of those children lived at the hospital for six months with terrible illnesses including, God forbid, cancer.

I saw our situation in a new light. We were the lucky ones. The experience really opened my eyes. We take good health for granted, but it's everything. We walked out of that hospital appreciating our family so much. I couldn't leave the feeling behind, so I started to donate to children's hospitals. With St. Joseph's in Paterson, I do Christmas toy drives and help raise funds.

I also do a lot of work with Deborah Hospital in Brown Mills, New Jersey. As a young kid, I had open-heart surgery there. I was seven and had the blood pressure of an 80-year-old woman. It was coarctation of the aorta. It's a congenital narrowing of the main artery of the heart. I stayed at the hospital for a month. For whatever reason, our family didn't have heath insurance in the 1980s. Only people who had regular jobs or were rich had it. My surgery would have cost hundreds of thousands of dollars. At Deborah Hospital, they don't turn anyone away. If it weren't for the good people there, I have no idea what would have happened to me. I still have a huge scar across my back from that surgery. I forget about the scar, but people walk up to me and tell me I have a scratch on my back. My mom fought with the doctors to cut through my back so I wouldn't have a huge scar on my chest when I got older.

Gino's stay in the hospital brought it all back for me. But this time, I was in my mother's chair by the bed. Joe and I were in the midst of our financial crisis at the same time, too. But I swear, I never felt more blessed to have my family than when we were at our lowest.

Our children are the literal and figurative products of our love. When you make a baby and look at the person you created together, the marital bond only grows. I know Joe would love to have more kids, but I think my baby-making days are over. I always wanted to have three, and feel blessed and very lucky to have our three beautiful loving children. Three C-sections was enough for my body.

As they get older, I look back at their baby days nostalgically. I was exhausted constantly, but I miss that time. Before we know it, they'll be teenagers. Can't wait to see how Joe handles it when Antonia brings home her first boyfriend! I feel sorry for the kid already. Stay tuned. That'll be a juicy one.

PARENTING ITALIAN STYLE

WHAT WE SAY GOES

Early on, I made a ruling on an issue. I don't remember what it was, it could have been staying up late or eating cookies before dinner. I said "no." The kids went to Joe, and he said "yes." He contradicted me. I said to him, "You just taught the kids that what I say means nothing. That can't happen again." And it hasn't. We parent as a single unit. Joe and I have to come to an agreement before making any decisions. As a rule, we don't talk about the matter at hand in front of them. The kids understand that if they upset me, they upset Joe. "Don't get Mommy mad, or you'll get me mad," he says. The kids can't back down fast enough.

SHOW AND TELL

You don't see our kids too often on RHONJ. We try our hardest not to have the story line have much to do with them. They're simply too young. We want to limit their abnormal experiences. And, believe me, having a camera in their faces, a crew trailing them around the house and to their activities is not normal for a five-year-old. When the cameras are off, however, our kids are front and center. In some families, when Daddy comes home, the children get out of sight. Absolutely not in this household. We sit down at the dinner table together as often as possible. We talk to them, and make them talk to us. We believe children should be seen and heard. They're encouraged to speak their minds, use words carefully and clearly. But no back talk. I'm not afraid to reprimand my children in front of people.

KIDS ARE A JOY, EVEN WHEN
THEY DRIVE YOU NUTS

When Antonia was a baby, I became a full-time mom. In four years, we had three kids. I was at home with them from 6:00 A.M. to 9:00 P.M. Joe would come home covered in dirt head to toe. No matter how tired I was, or how filthy he was, I was so glad to see another adult. I'd sit and chat about his day, the kids, and upcoming plans. I kept my tone light and my voice smooth. Of course, I was tired and stressed out. I was home with three babies all day long! I felt the temptation to unload my stress on him, to nag and complain. But that wouldn't turn my feelings around, or make him feel glad to see his kids. We'd both worked as hard as we could. He'd been sweating at construction sites for twelve hours. He needed peace when he got home. I needed it, too. I wanted to relax into his presence and companionship. Bitching was the opposite of relaxing. Hugs and kisses would calm me down. A whining contest would wind me up.

Some guys change one diaper or give a baby one bottle, and declare themselves Super Dad. They hand the baby back to Mommy, and then go to the garage to putter around or sneak off to their office to look at porn. I don't feed babies, or change the diapers. My father never wiped my ass, and I don't wipe my babies' either. But, I get on the floor and play with my kids for hours.

DOUBLE STANDARDS

My father was strict. No boys were allowed in the house, or to call the house either. I wasn't allowed to go to the mall with my girlfriends unless I had a reason—and "just to hang out" was not going to cut it. He'd grill me whenever I left the house. "Where are you going? What are you doing? Who with?" I'm a terrible liar. I had to walk a straight line just so I wouldn't get caught in a lie.

Joe is just as strict with Antonia, and it's going to get even worse. During any kissing scenes on their TV shows, he makes her cover her eyes. He's funny about boys and kissing, anything sexual at all. She is not allowed to see it. Antonia won't be allowed to have boyfriends come over. Even when she's in her twenties, Joe and I do not want to know. I know Antonia is going to have them, but we want her to respect herself. That means making her realize how seriously we take the matter of boys and sex.

My sons can have a separate entrance to the house. They can come and go as they wish. They can have anyone up to their room. I don't care. But I want to keep Antonia my little girl. Look, I know she's going to meet someone one day, and it's going to happen. But not with fifteen people!

My wish is for her to have one boyfriend for a very long time. They have a mutual breakup with no bad feelings. Then she marries the next guy. That would be ideal. I don't want her to ever have her heart broken. The only way I can see to helping her romantic life work out that way is be really strict and overprotective about who she sees, when she goes out, and what she does.

I know it's a double standard. But I just don't care! I don't see it so much as restricting Antonia, but as protecting her.

KEEP IT CLEAN

They know the rules. No food upstairs. Clean their own rooms. Put away their toys. Even at three years old, Joey knows that if he takes a toy out, he has to put it back when he's done with it. I'm a real stickler for straightening. I'd go crazy with toys and pieces of clothing scattered all over the house. I might be passing along my compulsion for neatness to my kids. But one day, when they have their own houses and find themselves doing the dishes and making it look nice, they'll be grateful they learned at a young age the value of order. I'm also teaching them to respect me. They know I keep house. If the kids didn't have to help me, they'd see me as someone who ran around picking up after them, and not as the authority figure who teaches them how to take care of themselves.

You can bend a tree when it's a seedling. But when that tree grows into an oak that's ten feet wide, you can't bend it. That's why we're on our kids from a very young age. We spend a lot of time with them to teach them how to behave and what our values are.

My father gave me that saying about the tree. He gave me everything I instill in my kids. What I learned growing up about respect and loyalty is what I teach my family. My father treated my mother like a queen, and I treat Melissa that way. He taught me to live well and work hard. I followed in his footsteps, and my kids will follow in mine.

DON'T BABY YOUR SPOUSE

Growing up, I was the baby of the house. With two older sisters, I always felt like I had three moms. I was the show doll. They'd dress me up, and do anything to make me feel better when I was upset. I was showered with attention and always felt incredibly loved. I said, "Watch me, watch me!" and everyone did. When I cried, I was wrapped in hugs and given candy.

Joe treats me like a grown woman, and expects me to behave like one. If I cry over a small thing, like a Tweet from a hater, Joe tells me to forget about it. He has no patience for getting upset about something meaningless. He was brought up hardcore. He was not allowed to let unimportant things get him down. When I was pregnant and grouchy, he didn't want to hear about it. But, if I cry about missing my father, Joe is the first one to squeeze me tight, and wipe my tears.

He acknowledges the emotions that matter. He's quite the crier himself, actually. I take some credit for that. When we first met, he was like Mussolini. It was a big job for me to tone down his swagger. As much as he's toughened me up, I've smoothed out his rough edges. Compromise in a marriage is so much bigger than deciding where to have dinner or what car to buy. It's how you bend your behavior to meet each other's needs and make each other happy.

I could have married a man who treated me like a child. But I married Joe. He doesn't let me get away with acting like a brat. If he did, I wouldn't know who I am, and what I'm capable of. When a grown woman is treated like a child, her potential is lost.

PART FOUR

· ·

Puttana in the Bedroom

I saved the best part for last. It's no secret that Joe is a sexually voracious man and a throw-down lover. Thank you, JESUS!

To be a *puttana* in marriage, a woman needs to keep herself in shape. She has to be seductive. She must be willing to try new things for her husband's pleasure and her own. And, most important, she has to be available for sex.

The way I see it, if a wife is a puttana, her husband will never feel the urge to go outside the marriage to actual whores, or strip clubs. He won't hit on women in bars, or drool over his friend's girlfriends or the secretary. He'll rush home to his wife, who makes sure he'll have a good time (the *best* time) in the comfort of his own home.

The bedroom should feel like a boudoir, with sensual fabrics and sumptuous colors. You don't need to go over the top with nude paintings and marble sculptures of Venus and Cupid. You certainly don't need bright red satin sheets. But thick luxurious carpeting can turn the barefoot walk from the bathroom to the bed into an erotic journey. A neat uncluttered boudoir gives it a sensual purpose. Turn the TV off. No cell phones, and definitely no computers, unless, that is, you and your man have a predilection for porn.

A man will never go outside his marriage for sex unless he's not getting it at home. I know a guy whose wife refused to do it. He wound up cheating. They went to a psychiatrist to try to work things out. My friend told the shrink everything. The wife agreed. She said she had no interest in sex, and wasn't going to change. After a few sessions, the psychiatrist flat out said, "I got no help for you, buddy." A couple that stops having sex needs help. But if the wife won't change, they're beyond it.

Sex is a marital lubricant. When you have lots of it, the little things slide. I can do something that pisses him off on Monday, but if we had sex on Sunday night, it blows over more easily. But if we haven't done it for two days and I give him attitude? It could be a huge fight. Besides, it's a medical necessity for us to have sex every other day. If we didn't, Joe's unreleased poison would kill him (at least, that's what he tells me . . .).

CHAPTER THIRTEEN

· ·

Well-Oiled Sex Machine

I'm proud of how I look, and not embarrassed to say so. Caring about your looks is superficial only if you do it for shallow reasons. I work on my outside to gain confidence on the inside. It gives me a pop when I get in front of the camera or on stage. I do it to feel healthy and strong. Being attractive turns me on. I work hard on my body; Joe loves my body. When we're in bed, he objectifies *the hell* out of me—and I love every minute of it. In or out of bed, I want to feel like I'm the best thing he's ever seen. I want his eyes on me. Being his sex object takes effort. I put in the time, and reap the rewards.

There is a difference between pretty and sexy. Men want sexy. Every woman can be sexy if she wants to. It's all in the attitude, how you feel about yourself and how you carry yourself.

> I love Melissa's body! I can't get enough of her all night long.

I love Joe's body, too. I can't keep my hands off his chest. Everyone thinks Joe gets his bulging muscles from pumping iron at the gym. He does work hard for them, but the majority come from construction and picking up heavy materials. He still gets in there. It turns me on to know a lot of his hot body comes from hard work. He gets his cardio in the bedroom. Although I don't love it when he gets completely naked on the show, which he has done too many times, you can see what I mean. (In a certain mood, he can't keep his clothes on! Once a stripper, always a stripper.) And yes, he calls himself Tarzan. Ugh.

You don't have to be gorgeous, thin, and perfect to be sexy. The man who loves you does not care if you've gained ten pounds. But he will care if those ten pounds make you so self-conscious and uptight that you can't relax, strut your stuff, throw off your clothes, and have fun in bed. If you're obsessing about your fat belly or thick thighs, then it's impossible to let sensations sweep you away. For a woman to respond the way she and her husband both want—to feel red hot and ready—she's got to love her own body, or at least be able to put those negative thoughts aside. Sexy is an attitude. Find your Sasha Fierce.

I used to be the queen of excuses. I'd say to myself, "Oh, I don't need to go to the gym and sweat. I don't really feel like it. I don't have time." Those days are behind me. I'm not twenty anymore. I'm thirty-three, and have had three kids. My body doesn't quite bounce back like it used to. I'm only 5 feet 4 inches tall, and if I gain five pounds, it shows. I used to rely on genes and being naturally petite. Now I rely on sweat. When you work out, everything tightens up and starts to tone. By "tone," I don't mean rock hard with chiseled abs. Joe likes me to be soft and curvy, but tight and slim. If I expect him to get hard for me, I can get firm for him.

How to love your own body? Like everything, true love springs from a deep understanding. You've got to know yourself. I don't mean just being able to locate and identify all of your parts, below and above the waist. Body awareness comes from use. I firmly believe in the connection between exercise, healthy food, and great sex. Treat your body like a sex machine, that needs to be lovingly maintained, oiled, and polished and you will immediately notice a big shift in how you feel. Believe me, if you take excellent care of your body, you will want someone else to appreciate it with his words and eyes, and his hands (and other parts). It all starts with you. You are in control of your body. You're in control of your sex life.

My kids are my cardio, but a little running helps, too.

FITNESS ITALIAN STYLE

The fitness-sex connection can't be underestimated. If you exercise your body, you are better in bed. Developing muscles, and increasing stamina and flexibility will make you a better lover. You can get into more positions, and go longer. Aerobic exercise pushes oxygen through your body. It goes all the way to the surface of your skin, making it healthier and more sensitive to the touch. And then there are all the emotion benefits of fitness. You feel good because you look good. You're refreshed.

When I'm in great shape, I glide through life. My skin glows. I have tons of energy. The feeling can't be beat.

Joe and I sometimes work out together. Watching each other sweat is a turn on. Anything physical we share gets us going. Joe tends to do his arms. I want to work on my legs. He's over there doing his thing, I'm over here doing my thing. We watch each other in the mirror. It's sexy. I know he's doing his workout to look great for me, and vice versa. We push each other to our limit for each other's benefit. And once in a while, if we're lucky enough to get away from the kids, we jump in the shower, and have the best sex. Lots of soap! Remember my OCD.

The couple that pumps together . . .

IF IT'S NOT JOE, IT'S GYM

I work out with a trainer or go to the gym three times a week. I drop the kids off and drive straight there. I have to do it in the beginning of the day or it won't happen. Since I run around with the kids all day, and up and down stairs like a human taxi, I consider that my cardio. So at the gym I do a lot of toning—lunges, squats, and lifting. When I feel laziness coming on—*I'll skip today and double my workouts next week*—I tell myself, it's only an hour. That's why I like group exercise classes. When you're with a crowd, it keeps you going.

MIND-SET

I don't like the phrase "problem areas." I'd rather think of certain parts as having "room for improvement." You will never hear me say that I hate any part of myself. My philosophy is to love yourself, and one way you do it is pay special attention to the parts you might be inclined to pretend didn't exist at all.

MIDSECTION

I've always had a tiny waist. After having Joey a few years ago, I had to focus a lot harder on my stomach. Things I used to rely on aren't guaranteed. Joe and I go down the shore a lot during the summer, and I live in my bikini. My stomach is out there for anyone to see. During those months, I double my sit-ups and work more on my core. My trainer has me do every crunch known to man—standard, obliques, and bicycles with and without a medicine ball. Leg lifts get at my lower abs, the ones south of the belly button. I also do a lot of planks for my entire core. They look easy, but after sixty seconds, my whole body shakes.

KEGELS

Call me crazy, but I really think Kegels help. This is one muscle group you can't ignore! I remember reading about Kegels in magazines when I was a teenager. The articles always said the same thing. You've heard it before. Repeat after me: Squeeze your pelvic floor muscles like you're stopping the flow of pee. Hold for ten seconds. Relax. Repeat ten times. Do it every day. It sounds like bullshit. But it's the real deal. Squeezing brings blood to your parts, making them more sensitive. And the added benefits that you feel like you're getting a lower ab workout the whole time. Joe doesn't mind the squeezing either.

ARMS

I don't use more than ten to twelve pound weights. If you lift heavier weights, you might bulk up and look less feminine. The key word is "tone" not "tough." Some trainers would say that ten pounds is too much for women. I do bicep curls, tricep kickbacks, rows, shoulder and chest presses.

LEGS

My inner and outer thighs seem almost impossible to tone. I have to work double time on them, and hate it.

TUSH

Squats, squats, squats. And then, when I can't stand to do another, more squats. I also love vintage Jane Fonda moves, like lying on my side and lifting the top leg. I will try anything that will make my tush look lush. I know a lot of women try to make their ass smaller. I'm trying to make mine bigger. The bigger the better.

THINGS NOT TO DO IN FRONT
OF YOUR HUSBAND
. . . .

Double standard alert. Joe can and does a lot of the things on this list in front of me. I don't necessarily like it, but I give him a pass. He's part animal anyway. But I was raised to keep my bodily functions to myself. Ladies are discreet about such things. It goes back to the idea of dating your husband. On a first date, would you let out a huge belch? On a second date, you would let it rip in bed? Not on your life. Don't let politeness die, and never let him see you . . .

1. **Poop.** Moms, you all know the book *Everyone Poops*, right? It's wrong. Girls don't poop. Me, never have. Never will. It just doesn't happen. Or, that's what Joe thinks! We've been married for nine years, and he has never once seen or smelled my business. How have I pulled this off? I don't do it when he's around or awake. In an emergency, I have my ways of pooping so he won't hear, smell, or see. It's a challenge. Joe has asked me, in complete seriousness, "Do you poop?" He can't catch me. He always tries. He springs in on me when I've been in the bathroom for a while, only to find me tweezing my eyebrows. Ha!

2. **Fart**. I like to call it *puff*. The only time I would puff in front of Joe would be outside, in a tornado, with him wearing noise-cancelling headphones and a clothespin on his nose.

3. **Change a tampon**. I have no words. I can't even. This is not okay. Just NO. Talk about destroying the mystery. And don't forget to flush them, please! When men see blood, they think something died.

4. **Pick** . . . your nose, your eye gunk, an ingrown hair. A lady does not dig for gold. I'm grossed out when Joe cleans house in front of me.

BODY IMAGE AND DIET
ITALIAN STYLE

Sex is about sensual pleasure. So is eating and loving food. All sensual input flows in the same direction. Put a roadblock on food, then you're jamming up the sexual signals, too. Italians believe having a healthy appetite for food translates into a hearty appetite for sex as well.

We also believe "diet" is the four-letter word. Just eating right is a lot easier than telling yourself that, for two weeks, you can have this and you can't have that. As soon as you swear off something, it becomes the one thing you can't stop thinking about. You'll make yourself crazy. You might lose weight in those two weeks of suffering, but most people gain it all back, and a few more pounds on top of it for your trouble. Dieting brings up negative emotions, like guilt (if you cheat), depression (if you gain the weight back), and anger (at yourself).

As it pertains to marriage, I've seen couples take a nosedive when the wife goes on a diet. She turns into a snarling bitch because she's starving and grumpy. He's annoyed that he can't relax and eat his favorite foods. The next thing you know, there's resentment on both sides that builds into a fight, or worse, a fester. Forget about sex. That's no way to live, love your husband, or treat yourself.

I eat healthily and use portion control. If my clothes start to feel small, I have the same food, but put less on my plate. I stay active. I'm not the girl who sits around the house all day eating snacks. I'm always on the go and running from place to place with my kids. Eating healthily with portion control is how to live well everyday. It's not a chore. It's good for you and feels good.

TURN IT OFF

If you do one thing to lose weight—and I know this might sound strange, coming from me—turn off the TV. I swear, television makes you fat. You watch those food commercials when you're tired and vulnerable. You're sitting on your ass. Instead, get your mind off junk and be active. I only watch an hour of TV at night before bed. I always have fruit next to me, or otherwise I'd go for the cupcakes and ice cream. At least three nights a week, I eat pomegranates; I put a napkin on my lap because the juice stains.

NIBBLE

Hunger is what drives people to pig out. You starve to the point of mania, and then inhale the contents of the fridge. I never let myself get too hungry. I eat a lot more than three times a day. Between meals, I have a piece of fruit. When you snack almost exclusively on fruit, that's what you crave. If you snack on chips and cookies, that's what you'd crave. They say it takes six months to make a habit. With fruit, it's way faster. Keep a bowl full of apples, oranges, or grapes on your table, and two months later, that's all you'll want.

DIVIDE AND CONQUER

If I buy a treat that comes in a package of two, like cupcakes, I eat one, and put the other away for another day. Same with, say, a brownie. Cut it in half, love the hell out of every bite, and save the rest for another time. I never go crazy craving sweets because I eat them every day. This might be the one area of my life that I'm satisfied with a tiny bit of a great thing.

BREAKFAST

Light, light, light. Some people can eat a big breakfast and get on with their day. Not me. I just have my tea or coffee and a piece of toast or a small bowl of cereal. That's usually all I have time for before getting the kids up, dressed, and out the door to school.

LUNCH

I like something delicious. Big flavor, small quantity. If I ate a huge meal in the middle of the day, it'd slow me down. With three young kids, I can't afford to lose a step. I have a turkey or tuna sandwich. A salad with some protein in it, like cheese or grilled chicken.

DINNER

As I said several chapters ago, I cook at home as often as possible. A typical weekday dinner for the family is a piece of meat, rice or potatoes, and a vegetable. Joe and I shy away from carbs during the week. The kids get the carbs. Joe and I put just a taste on our plate. I never want to feel deprived. I add vegetables to dishes to make them healthier. For example, a recipe I've been making a lot lately is chicken breast sliced really thinly with bruschetta—diced fresh tomatoes, garlic, parsley and olive oil—on top, with a drizzle of white wine. Or chicken cutlets with fresh spinach, garlic and oil on top. So easy, so delicious, and super healthy.

FAST FOOD

If I eat fast food, it's going to be the good stuff—*pizza*. I eat one slice probably three days a week. In the Olympics of fast food, pizza gets the gold medal. It's made with fresh ingredients, including tomato sauce and mozzarella cheese. It's not fried or made with chemicals I can't pronounce. Again, it's all about portion control. I have just one slice—and no greasy pepperoni!

LIQUID CALORIES

No soda! I don't drink juice or sugary drinks. I drink seltzer with lemon all day long. As far as alcohol goes, I don't drink much during the week. But when I go out for a drink on a Saturday night with Joe, it's usually just one or two. Why drink your calories? I'd rather eat them!

DATE NIGHT

No reservations when Joe and I are out at a restaurant on Saturday nights. I like to enjoy, but I do tend to get a piece of meat and a vegetable. We always share a dessert.

CAKE!

Homemade box cake is my weakness. If I can have a little sliver at the end of every night, I'm happy.

SPLURGE DAY

On Sundays, I eat anything I want. All bets are off. There are no rules. I never go completely overboard. For breakfast, I eat whatever my little heart desires. By 2:00 P.M., we're eating pasta, bread, and all the foods that are the perks of being Italian.

HERE COMES THE GROOM

It's not enough to keep my body toned and slim. I also keep myself very well groomed. In the pre-marriage days, before a date, women groom obsessively. Wax the bikini. Nair the 'stache and shave the pits. Exfoliate and moisturize. Get a spray tan. Brush and floss teeth. Then buff, polish, and paint themselves to feel sexy and sleek for their new boyfriend.

Then, after a few years of marriage, things slip. Women shave less frequently. They let their skin get dry. It's not that a loving husband will suddenly feel repulsed by armpit stubble and bad breath . . . actually, he will. But because he loves you and doesn't want to hurt your feelings, he won't bring it up. He might not complain, but that doesn't mean he's not thinking *Ewwww*.

Keep love alive. Use deodorant.

Joe would say something if my garlic breath was too much. So I don't give him anything to complain about. Listen ladies, even if it's the thousandth time, you need to act like it's the first time that you're having sex with your husband, and clean up your act. Of course, you're not going to manage it *every* time. But don't wait until you're divorced to tune up your body. Do it now. Do it for yourself, and for your husband, and your marriage. Trust me, he'll notice.

CHAPTER FOURTEEN

Our Version of Foreplay

One of my favorite expressions is, "The grass isn't greener on the other side, it's greener where you water it." Every gardener knows that if you don't pay attention to a part of the lawn, it'll dry up and die. But if you give it the attention it needs, it'll thrive. You have to water your romantic life to keep it healthy! Give it a good soak. Tend to it every day, in some small way, and it'll bloom and grow. Stop looking at your friends and other people's marriages and start watering your own.

Joe and I keep up the romance with extended foreplay. Our version of foreplay isn't what we do before intercourse. It's what we do to create sexual tension between us before we even get in the bedroom. We're engaged in foreplay all day long. Even when I walk past him and give him the eye makes him think about what's going to happen later. This might not happen every day. Yes, I have three kids and I'm working round the clock, but I still find time for a two-second wink.

SEDUCTION ITALIAN STYLE

Marriage without passion isn't marriage. It's friendship. The stress of life makes couples fall out of the habit of flirting with each other. And forget about seduction! That takes too much planning and work. I hear my friends complain, "Why should I make the effort for his sake? He never tries to seduce me!"

If you don't know by now, I don't believe in score keeping or tit-for-tat. He doesn't seduce you, so you refuse out of spite? How will that turn the tide in your relationship? Since the days of Salome and Cleopatra, seduction has been a woman's job. We use our wiles, and in return, our men worship us like Goddesses. If pride gets in the way of that, both partners suffer. Instead, do one or two small things to let him know you're thinking about him in *that* way, and he'll be eager, willing, and able to follow your lead and repay your seduction tenfold. You have every right to have pride outside in the workplace, but when you come home, lose the pride.

Seduction really doesn't require much effort. A certain look.

A small touch. Most men are like pilot lights, always ready to burst into flame. They just need a blast of romantic fuel. How I do it:

GIVE GOOD SEXT

I send Joe a flirty text while he's at work once or twice a week. Often enough that it's not shocking, but not too often that he gets used to it. One part humor, two parts naughty. It's just supposed to make his eyes light up as he reads it. I wouldn't write anything that would make me die of shame if someone read it over his shoulder. I never send photos. I don't trust him not to show someone. For example:

"I'm wearing red underwear. Early dinner tonight?"

"You have no idea what I'm going to do to you when you get home."

Don't be shy! This is your husband. Even if you just say, "I want you," he'll rush home.

WARM WELCOME

A half-an-hour before Joe's arrival, I change out of my baggy sweats and slip into tight yoga pants and a cute top. I brush my teeth, freshen up my makeup and brush my hair. Maybe a spritz of perfume. When he comes in, I kiss him hello and give him a smile. He feels bathed in the warm welcome, and any lingering work stress dissipates. Changing a man's mood is the essence of seduction. It's using your smile, eyes, and soft touch to shift his mind away from the world and his problems and onto you.

SHOW TIME

When Joe sits at the table and watches me cook dinner, I can feel his eyes on me. To make sure they stay there, I tease him by bending a certain way. I can hear his breath catch from across the room.

> Men are visual creatures. If we see something we like, we attack. A lion sees a gazelle, he attacks. His jowls are dripping and he can't wait to tear at that gazelle with his teeth. But he'll wait for a while, just watching it. His appetite is stimulated through his eyes. Watching first prolongs the thrill of the hunt.

I really give him a show before we go out on the weekends. I love trying on outfits for Joe. It's a little bit of pre-dinner flirting. Flirting is *never* a bad thing. "Don't I look cute?" I ask, looking for compliments. I know what Joe likes. If a dress is body conscious, and shows off my legs, he's sure to have a moment.

> A husband has needs. A wife has needs. You have to be united in the desire to do for each other. It's the small things. My wife likes this cologne. I want to be sexy for her, so I wear it. It happens to smell good. But even if it made me stink, I'd still wear it.

INHALE

We know from animals that smell is a powerful way to connection. A mother cat knows her kittens by their scent alone. Whether you realize it or not, people connect by smell, too. Scent to me is everything. My olfactory sense is sharp. I sniff peaches to find the best one, I smell my kids when they walk by me. And I sniff Joe's neck every chance I get. Call me crazy, but that's what I do when I love something. When Joe's not around, I smell his shirt and miss him terribly. I think scent inspires passion as much as visual triggers. Looking good is one thing. But smelling good? That goes deep. We each have our signature scent that we've been wearing for each other for ten years, too.

REACH OUT AND TOUCH

Joe says I'm "touchy feely." He wouldn't have it any other way! I touch him whenever he's near enough on his arms, his shoulders, his neck. We hold hands, and put our arms around each other. We are basically in each other's back pockets. I lure Joe into touching me with any excuse. I ask him to rub my sore muscle after a workout, or to put lotion on my legs. He jumps at the chance to moisturize my feet. He's got a tiny foot fetish. (Another reason I'm obsessed with pedicures.)

Now, some men don't like to be grabbed and touched. They feel crowded. You don't have to cling like a monkey. Just a one-second touch on his arm when you talk. A hand on his leg under the table. A rub on his back. Touching thighs on the couch while you chill in the evenings. The key word is *affection*. Loving touches connect you on an emotional and physical level. When you get in bed, you gravitate toward each other naturally and comfortably. When couples don't touch outside of bed, the pressure goes way up when they get in there. A woman might start to feel used if the only time her husband touches her is when he wants sex. Women need affection! Men do, too. They want that confirmation that their woman is drawn toward them and can't keep her hands to herself.

CHAPTER FIFTEEN

· ·

Full-Body Gorgasm

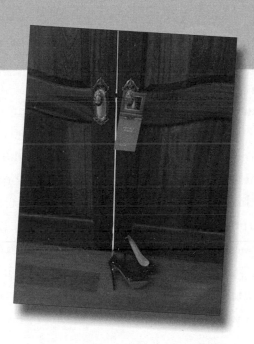

Men are easy to please. As long as the woman in their bed is into it, they're thrilled. Enthusiasm and desire trump crazy and freaky every time. Magazines will churn out article after article, year after year, with sex tips. Hey, I'm a big fan of learning new things. Those stories can turn into a fun night or two. We've found a few keepers over the years. But the old ways of making love are what we always seem to go back to. You could make a list of a hundred "mind-blowing" sex tricks, but none of them will have the same physical and emotional impact as a hot kiss, looking each other in the eye, and moving to the rhythm that is just right for the two of you.

I'm not going to get too graphic here. I'm a lover, but I'm also a mother. If you want to read about the real down and dirty, you'll have to go somewhere else. What I'm here to tell you is that it doesn't really matter how we or you do it. Every couple has their own style. Every person has his and her own turn-ons and offs. But there are aspects to sex Joe and I do want to share.

I did a survey of my friends and looked around online, and my theory turns out to be true. For the most part, men fantasize about doing things to women (often more than one; threesomes are the most common sexual fantasy!). Women fantasize about men doing things to them, in different settings and in different outfits. So it works out perfectly. Men have that instinctual urge to dominate, and women, whether they realize it or not, want to submit. The point is: Men want to be men; women want to be women. Husbands want their wives to submit; wives to want our husbands to dominate. For this reason, we . . .

PLAY CATCH

All men love the idea that a woman is good to go. But they don't want it to be too easy. They want a challenge. They love it. If I didn't give Joe a hard time as much as I do, he wouldn't want it as much. I play hard to get—but not too hard. You don't want him to get pissed. I strut around the bedroom in skimpy clothes for fifteen minutes, letting him get a long look at me. Rarely, I pull out the big guns and walk out of the bathroom without a towel. He'll jump and grab me, Tarzan style. What woman doesn't want her husband to grab her for a throw down? It's always hottest when he has to come and get me. I might even make him chase me around the bed once or twice. I'm the Queen of playing hard to get. I love to tease.

BUSS STOP

After nine years of marriage, a lot of couples skip kissing entirely. But when they first started out, they spend hours on the couch just kissing, and it was the greatest, most sensual time of their lives. Look, no one with kids and a job has time for marathon make-out sessions. But kissing for five minutes really gets the butterflies going. Joe and I kiss all the time, in and out of bed. We have mini-makeouts nearly every time we see each other again after being apart. Not like we buss after a trip to the bathroom. But we do kiss when he comes home, when I've been away for an appearance. It's more intimate than sex to touch mouths, press your faces together, and breathe each other's air.

ORAL

I mean *talking*! The traditional definition of "open marriage," is when a husband and wife allow each other to have sex with other people. (FYI: That is *never* going to happen in our marriage. No. Cheating is unacceptable. We will never have a threesome. Our sex is between us, and that's it.) Our version of "open marriage" means open communication, especially about sex. We are completely free to say anything to each other. It's highly instructive. I know so much about how Joe's mind works because he tells me! He's so vocal, I never have to guess what he wants or how he feels. He explains it exactly, in minute detail. It means so much for him that I want to learn. I never have to ask, "How's this? Higher? Lower?" He tells me, and I comply. Put your pride down. I do it for Joe. And he does it for me, although it's hard for me to talk about intimate things. Joe always asks, "What do you want?" It's awkward, and the only time I get shy. I start to giggle. If I finally manage to get it out, Joe falls on the request like a ton a bricks. He is so eager to make me happy that I have to laugh sometimes.

For women, it can feel awkward and embarrassing to say what you want in the bedroom. It's been hard for me to do it. I just feel funny about it. But I try because I know Joe likes it, and because even the smallest quietest comment can be the difference between a little "oh" and a capital "O!!!"

DIRTY TALK

Sometimes Joe will ask me to repeat things he says or to talk dirty. My face turns red. I start to giggle. It's so hard to get it out. I know Joe loves it, but it comes out like a schoolgirl instead of a hot sexy woman. Practice makes perfect. If you can do it, good for you. I'm sure your man will love it.

DON'T MAKE YOUR HUSBAND FEEL LIKE A PERV

A man's mind can come up with some kinky ideas. It doesn't mean he's a twisted degenerate to bring it up with his wife. Don't judge his sexual fantasies. Just listen. Who knows? I might like a weird idea. I would rather listen to his request, figure out a way to satisfy him, and enjoy it myself, instead of his finding another woman who will.

We've been married nine years, with three kids. Sex is going to get boring after a while. You have to make an effort to keep a man's interest by putting on something sexy. Even a hot pair of underwear I haven't seen before gets me excited. If I said, "Wear that T-shirt to bed tonight with nothing else," Melissa knows exactly what to do. It goes both ways. If she asked me to walk around the bedroom with a G-string up my butt, I'd do that for her. It'd be fun, like a return to my stripper days when I worked at Chippendale's. Unfortunately, she never requests that. To keep a marriage going, you have to talk about every single thing. My wife is my life. I live to make her happy. I like it when she tells me what she wants.

RUSH JOB

Sometimes, all we have is a few minutes for sex. A quickie during halftime of a football game takes five to fifteen minutes. Just that snippet of time can make a huge difference in how the weekend goes. One thing I know from my own experience—and a lot of my friends tell me the same—is that if you haven't had sex for a couple of days, a little argument becomes a bigger deal. A small complaint gets overexaggerated. But, when Joe and I have sex a couple nights in a row, little fights don't seem so big. Happy guys let more go. Issues get brushed off. Quickies count. Say what you want, but it's the truth.

I hear guys at work and at the gym who say flat out, "If my wife would have sex for ten minutes, I wouldn't be so pissed off. Why does she have to be so selfish?"

She's not in mood to have sex? How about a three-minute massage instead? Men need to be touched. Skin on skin. A kiss, a hug, a massage. That's enough on some nights. If you can find the energy to hug your man for three minutes, you might change your mind about skipping sex for another ten.

YOU CAN DO JUST ABOUT ANYTHING FOR TEN MINUTES

Even when I'm exhausted and not really in the mood, if it means a lot to Joe that we connect physically, I'll say, "I'm not so into it tonight, but let's go." This goes back to the tenet of honesty. He wants to go, I could take it or leave it. But for ten minutes, it's fine. I tell him the truth. Of course, Joe wants me to be 100 percent into it. But let's get real, that doesn't happen all the time.

After a day running around with the kids, some nights I don't want anyone to touch me, not even Dr. McDreamy. If it's a hard "no," I try to be nice about it. Don't swat him away, or say with a tone, "Leave me alone!" Eventually, he will leave you alone a lot more than you wish he would. Most likely, he'll be fine with a rejection if you can give him some kindness and attention. Put yourself in his shoes. If your man snapped and gave you the cold shoulder to avoid sex, wouldn't that hurt your feelings? But if he gave you a kiss and hug, told you he loved you and promised to make it up to you tomorrow night, you'd roll over and be satisfied with that.

One of the ways my wife shows me respect is by making mad passionate love to me. When I knock on the door, it opens. Hey! I'm a thirty-eight-year-old man. I need sex! Every man does. I show my wife respect back by giving her what she wants. If I didn't, she'd feel unappreciated. Ladies, you know it's true. You feel prettier, sexier, and more loved if your man can't take his hands off you.

Ladies, read this part to your husbands. Men, I know you think your woman isn't the type who wants to be taken. But trust me, she is. Every girl wants to get her hair pulled once in a while. If your wife says "no," turn her around, and rip her clothes off. She wants to be dominated. Even if your wife is a tough, strong businesswoman who breaks balls all day long—especially in that case—when it's just the two of you, she wants to be dominated.

I gave this advice to a friend of mine. A week later, we went to their place for dinner. The husband pulls me to the side and whispers, "I took your advice. It's been amazing. I had her on the kitchen counter before you got here." His wife was glowing. She walked by him and kissed him on the cheek.

SOME STRANGE

When I gained weight during pregnancy, Joe was totally into it. He said it was like having sex with a different woman. He loves variety. Do what you can to seem like a different woman. Hair up, hair down. Be a little more aggressive one night, and passive to the point of timid the next. Be loud on Monday, and whisper on Wednesday. When you can surprise each other, passion keeps burning. Predictable is the enemy of sex.

You simply have to try new things, positions, and places. I don't mean you go to the extremes of having sex in the middle of the Short Hills Mall. I mean something as simple as, if you usually do it facing the headboard, next time, turn it around and face the foot of the bed. Little tweaks can make a huge difference.

Men like to change it up. I don't want filet mignon every night. Sometimes, I want a cheeseburger or a chili dog. Give me a menu to choose from, and I'll be happy. Women don't realize how easy men are. Just give us what we want, you can have everything we've got.

When Melissa gets into bed, she rubs her hands together, and wonders, *Who's Joe going to be tonight? Is he going to that guy who makes soft, sweet love to me or is he going to rip my clothes off and throw me around the room?*

I always keep her on her toes.

THE ULTIMATE SEX BOMB

. . . .

The only thing Joe and I absolutely won't do in bed?

Fake Gorgasm.

Never, ever, ever.

Joe accused me once of faking it. I was pretty loud and dramatic there at the finish. He said, "Was that real or did you fake?" The expression on his face—he looked so insulted and hurt.

I said, "No! Of course not!" Faking in bed is the worst kind of betrayal. Not only are you lying to your man, but you're cheating yourself.

Men's egos are wrapped up in pleasing woman. When she has an orgasm, he soars. When she doesn't, it's too bad, but whatever. It just gives the couple something awesome to look forward to and work towards. But if she fakes? He thinks he's Superman, and will keep doing the same old routine, and she dreads the thought of it. Faking reinforces bad sex.

Either way, faking is a major no-no. "Marriage is teamwork," as Joe says. "If she's not feeling it, she can just say so and take one for the team."

Quickies aren't that satisfying for me. I need to take my time. They're like Chinese food. An hour later, I want to go again. I'll come back as soon as possible for more, and Melissa says, "We just did it last night!" She's been saying that to me for ten years.

SLOW DOWN!

Sex is not a sprint to the finish! That is, unless you have kids barging into your room or falling asleep on your bed.

> The kids are constantly coming in our room. We've always got one in bed with us. They refuse to go back to their room, and then fall dead asleep. It'd take longer to wake them up and fight over getting them back to their room. Joey gets wired and then jumps on the bed.
>
> So we have to sneak out of our room and go into theirs. And then we have to be completely silent. It drives me insane. I'm thirty-eight. I don't want to have to make love to my wife by sneaking around in silence. It is what it is. Oh, the baby years. You gotta love it.

EYES OPEN

I read in *Cosmo* once that sex is better if you close your eyes and think of someone else. I can't imagine doing that. Isn't that cheating? That's not what we're doing here. Don't give into that. Open your eyes and be satisfied with what you've got. And if it's not perfect, you can work to make it better, rather than closing your eyes and wishing it away.

> When I make love to Melissa, I want her in the right mood and I'll do everything to get her there. I want her to be so satisfied, she'll never think about another man. I like my wife to fantasize about me. And I don't want to fantasize about another woman.

> That's what keeps our relationship real. I don't want her to want for anything. Anything she wants to do, we do it. If there's anything I want to do, we do it. Well, almost anything. Since we know we're going to get nearly anything we ask for, we don't have to worry about a craving going unsatisfied or being rejected.

Slumps do happen, even for us. There's real passionate sex and maintenance sex. You need them both for a healthy marriage. Maintenance sex keeps the wheels greased, the lines of communication open, and the fights to a minimum. Figure out what works for you in terms of frequency. Consider that number your required weekly amount. And then meet it!

Meeting your minimum isn't only for his sake. Once, when Joe was really overwhelmed with work, we went ten days without sex. On day five, I asked, "What, you're not touching me?" I admit, I was pissed and confused. By day eight, I started to lose it, yelling at him, "What are you doing behind my back!" No sex for over a week? It wasn't right. I started thinking about what he might be up to. It's not a good feeling. As soon as we got back on track, my mind quieted down. Couples owe each other that feeling of security. So whichever of you is temporarily off sex, remember that you owe it to your marriage to get back on.

A separated or newly divorced woman starts going to the gym, she gets her hair done, puts on makeup. I've got to wonder, *Why didn't you do that for your husband?* We have a friend, recently divorced. She got her boobs done, lost weight, bought a new wardrobe. She looks great! She's got a boyfriend and they have sex on the boat, in the car, like a young couple. I happen to know she doesn't really love the boyfriend. She still cries for her husband. So why didn't she please her husband and make it work while he was around? I'll tell you why. Couples fall into a bad pattern, a slump. They stop having sex, stop talking, and all of the sudden, they're done. Without the sex, a marriage is going to fall apart. What's a man going to do? Even if he loves his wife, he needs to feed.

CHAPTER SIXTEEN

· ·

Afterglow

T he second best part of sex (or the third) is the peaceful, quiet, satisfied calm afterwards. Since our lives are crazy busy, noisy, and hectic, we love the five minutes of bliss. Some nights, we cuddle for a long time. Other nights, we hold hands, breathe slowly and drift off the sleep. Sometime, a kid comes barreling into our room and we have to cover up and act like nothing kinky was just happening. Other times, I put my head on Joe's chest, and we zone out in front of the TV.

> Melissa is a cuddler. She won't get off me!

Guilty as charged. I love to be held in our warm cozy bed. I can't fall asleep unless Joe is in it next to me. If he's not there, I toss and turn all night. I'm physically incapable of sleeping without him. We must be touching, too. Some body part of mine has to be touching part of him. It's usually my foot on his leg.

> I know she's coming for it, so I position my foot for her to put hers on top. She's got this habit that she needs to make contact before sleep. She can't drift off unless she's anchored to me. I don't mind. I like it. Any touch from a woman shows a man, "I love you." That Melissa needs to touch me is proof of her love for me. The little things, touching toes, matter.

He's right. Joe is my anchor. Without him, I'd feel adrift. I don't care if that makes me sound needy or dependent. What's the point of a marriage if you don't depend on each other? That's why you get married in the first place—to have someone you count on no matter what.

I used to want to hold onto my independence, even after we got married. I didn't want to need anyone, not even Joe. Now, I know that it's arrogant to think you don't need anyone. Need is only a four-letter word if you don't accept it as another one: F-A-C-T. We *all* need love and support. The first person you should turn to for that basic human need is your partner, your better half, the man you lie down with at night and wake up with in the morning, the father of your children, your protector and provider, your soul mate, your confidant, your number one fan, and not-so-secret admirer.

I'm not a weaker woman for needing and depending on my husband. I'm stronger for it. We're a team. He's my best friend.

Epilogue: Valentine's Day 2013

St. Valentine was a priest in Rome around 270 AD. He was a Catholic during the era when most Romans believed in pagan Gods, which made him very unpopular with the powers that be. The Emperor at the time sentenced him to be locked up and put to death. His crime: He performed secret, illegal Christian sacraments for soldiers in the Roman army—including marriage. He risked and sacrificed his life so the Italian faithful could join body and soul with the women they loved. The day before his execution, Valentine sent a card—allegedly heart-shaped—to the daughter of his jailer who he cured of blindness (a miracle; hey, he was a saint). He signed it "From your Valentine." And the tradition of sending Valentine's Day cards was born.

Joe and I have been exchanging cards, gifts, and kisses for ten years. We've had hundreds of fights. Thousands! We've had three children together, and three rough pregnancies. We had 1,001 nights of quiet desperation during the recession. We got through five, white-knuckle days in the hospital when Gino was sick. For three years now, we've shared our lives on television. That's brought us a hundred highs, and just as many heartbreaks.

Through it all, the only number that really matters is one. Joe and I are united. We're individuals, but a single force. For every joy and sorrow we've been through together, we've grown closer. Writing this book has only reinforced my core belief, that merging your life with another person is the greatest blessing. I wish true passion, warm affection, and an Italian-style love for every one of you.

XOXO,
Melissa
February 14, 2013

Acknowledgments

As you all know, I'm big on expressing my gratitude. Good thing I've got so many people to thank for helping me with this book.

First and foremost, *Thank you, Jesus!* I speak to you every day and always have faith and trust in you to point me in the right direction.

Thank you, Joe! You're my inspiration, my support, my love, my protector, my everything. I'm so proud of who we are and what we've become together.

Thank you, Antonia, Gino, and Joey! My beautiful children, you're the reason I do everything. When I look at the three of you, my heart melts. There's no other happiness in the world greater than seeing you all smile.

Thank you to my mother Donna Marco and my sisters Lysa and Kim! My three moms! Without you, nothing would be possible. You love my kids like your own, and you give me peace of mind to leave them when I have to tear myself away.

Thank you to my grandmother, Nanny! You're always in my heart and soul. All of our long talks about my childhood came through in this book. I miss you immensely. Every time a butterfly goes by, I know it's you.

Thank you to my father, Anthony! You taught me the value of family and hard work. You're always in my heart and I will always love you.

Thank you, Andy Cohen and Bravo! You've given me a platform to share my life with so many people, and opened so many doors of opportunity. I'm forever grateful to you for inviting us on this wild ride.

Thank you, Jaime Cassavechia and Elizabeth Rosenthal Traub at EJ Media Group! You ladies always steer me in the right direction. Your advice and wisdom have been invaluable.

Thank you, Jessica Stark at MF Stark Group! You gave me the push to write *Love Italian Style*, and held my hand every step of the way. There'd be no book without you. So glad you're in my corner.

Thank you, Alex Glass at Trident Media Group! You were as good as an editor during the proposal stage and made the whole process fun and exciting.

Thank you, George Miguel! The best makeup artist in New Jersey! The saying is that beauty lies within. Thanks to your glam tips and expert technique, you really make it come out.

Thank you, Kathy Huck, John Murphy, and Kate Ottaviano, aka Team St. Martin's! What can I say? From the first meeting at my publishing house, I felt right at home. Kathy, you are an amazing editor. Thanks for your insight, ideas, and patience. John, I know you love Joe Gorga more than me, but I don't care. Your enthusiasm is infectious. Kate, thanks for all the support and staying on top of things.

· ACKNOWLEDGMENTS ·

Thank you, Valerie Frankel! Val, it has been wonderful working with you. We were totally in sync from the beginning. You're down-to-earth, and a pleasure to hang out with. I can't wait to get started on the next book!

$\mathcal{I}ndex$